MATT TOMPOROWSKI

How to Stop Being Toxic

10 Relatable Stories with Practical Lessons to Help You Break Toxic Habits and Build Healthy Relationships

"How to Stop Being Toxic: 10 Relatable Stories with Practical Lessons to Help You Break Toxic Habits and Build Healthy Relationships" is Book Three in the Book Series: "Let Go, Heal, Grow & Love" written by Matt Tomporowski

First edition

ISBN: 978-1-0689029-8-7

This book was professionally typeset on Reedsy.
Find out more at reedsy.com

To Xantha

Contents

Introduction

When an Ending Becomes a Beginning

Let me tell you something I never thought I'd say: I'm friends with my ex.

Yes—that ex. The one I was married to for over a decade. The one I shared a home with, built dreams with, and fought with when everything started to fall apart.

Our divorce happened during the pandemic, which I like to call the Great Relationship Filter. Some couples drew closer, while others, like us, unraveled. When she told me she wanted to end the marriage, I told myself I understood. I told myself I was okay. But the truth? I was devastated.

I didn't know it then, but that heartbreak cracked me open in a way that eventually let light in.

At first, the pain showed up as bitterness, blame, and reactivity. Our communication was laced with sarcasm, gaslighting, and old wounds being re-poked. We were two hurting people doing what hurting people often do, wounding each other further.

Looking back, I can admit it: I wasn't always kind. I wasn't always fair. And I didn't yet know what it meant to take ownership of my part in the dysfunction.

But something shifted after the dust settled. After we signed the papers, sold the house, and started living separately, something unexpected happened: peace. And over time, friendship.

What changed?

I gave myself space. I traveled. I walked through ancient ruins and hiked up sacred trails. And while my feet wandered, so did my mind. Sitting alone in airport lounges, watching the world pass by, I started to really see my patterns: the defensiveness, the emotional reactivity, the way I clung to control when I felt insecure.

I stopped needing to be right and started trying to understand. I practiced empathy—not just toward her, but toward myself. And through that process, I began to heal.

Today, my ex and I live just ten minutes apart. We check in, support each other's businesses, and sometimes grab coffee just to catch up. We're not trying to recreate the past. We're building something entirely new, rooted in respect and shared humanity.

That journey—from blame to accountability, from pain to peace—is what inspired this book.

What This Book Is Really About

This is not a book about saving relationships at any cost. It's about saving yourself from patterns that keep you stuck. Whether you're in a relationship now, recently out of one, or somewhere in between, this book is a guide to help you recognize and release toxic behaviors—both yours and others'—so you can build healthier, more fulfilling connections.

We'll explore

- how to recognize toxic behaviors, including the subtle ones that masquerade as "normal."
- why your attachment style may be running the show and how to stop letting it.
- tools for managing anxiety and overthinking so they don't hijack your relationships.
- communication techniques that are clear, kind, and grounded in truth.
- ways to heal past traumas without getting stuck in them.
- how to build emotional intelligence and respond instead of react.
- the art of setting and keeping boundaries without the guilt.
- empathy and compassion—what they really look like in practice.
- conflict resolution strategies that de-escalate instead of destroy.
- and finally, how to create a vision for the relationships you want and deserve.

Healing takes courage, growth takes honesty, and both take time.

But here's what I know for sure: Every step you take to understand your emotional patterns brings you closer to the relationships you're longing for. The kind that feel safe, respectful, and grounded in truth, not perfection.

You don't have to be flawless to be worthy of love. You just have to be willing to do the work.

So, whether you're standing in the rubble of a recent breakup, navigating a tough chapter in your current relationship, or realizing for the first time that maybe—just maybe—some of your behaviors need to shift... you're in the right place.

This isn't about shame. It's about choice. It's about breaking cycles, one conscious moment at a time. And it's about knowing that even when something ends, something else can begin— something deeper, truer, and infinitely more you.

It's time to stop being toxic. Are you ready for growth and healing?

1

Recognizing Toxic Behaviors

Harry spent 20 years in his first marriage. And if you'd asked him a few years ago why it ended, he would've told you that it was because his wife cheated. End of story, case closed.

But therapy has a funny way of peeling back the layers.

A couple of years in, Harry started to see the full picture. The uncomfortable, unedited version. The version where he wasn't just the betrayed husband but also the man who'd been quietly controlling, deeply rigid, and stuck in his ways. Harry grew up in a traditional household. His dad worked, and his mom stayed home, cooked, cleaned, and kept the house in perfect order. So, without really thinking about it, Harry carried that model into his marriage. He expected things to run the same way. And when they didn't? He didn't scream. He didn't rage. But he'd mutter, "Where's dinner?" or "Why isn't the laundry done?"—as if those comments weren't slowly eroding their connection. As if his wife wasn't a full human being with her own dreams, limits, and exhaustion.

After the divorce and the heartbreak, after therapy and reflection, something shifted.

He met someone new, and this time he knew she was the one. Engagement followed, and so did a new kind of fear: not of commitment, but of falling into old patterns. The last thing he wanted was for the ghosts of his unexamined behaviors to sabotage something real. So, Harry made a decision: He was going to do it differently this time. He was going to look in the mirror, face his blind spots, and build something healthier.

And that's what this chapter is about.

We've all heard the word "toxic" tossed around like confetti, whether on social media, in therapy memes, or whispered after a breakup. But toxic behaviors aren't always explosive or dramatic. They're often survival strategies we've outgrown. Coping mechanisms that once protected us but now hurt us. Scripts we inherited without realizing they were optional.

This chapter is not about blaming yourself or drowning in shame. It's about awareness, courage, and pressing pause long enough to ask yourself: *Are the ways I'm showing up in relationships growing love or pushing it away?*

It's time to unpack what these behaviors actually look like because they're not always loud or obvious. We'll explore where they come from, how to spot them, and how to shift. We'll talk about defensiveness, manipulation, emotional withdrawal, control, and more, but we'll do it in a way that feels doable and real.

Whether you're trying to heal a relationship, start a healthier one, or make peace with the past, this chapter will help you take the first step: holding the mirror, like Harry did, not to judge, but to change.

Let's begin.

Recognize Common Signs of Toxic Behavior

The first step in healing any toxic pattern is naming it. The truth is, many toxic behaviors don't come with flashing warning signs. They can show up in quiet habits or automatic reactions—things we've done for so long, we don't even question them. But when we take an honest look at how we act, especially in close relationships, we can start to shift from reaction to intention.

Here are common toxic behaviors that many of us (yes, even the most self-aware among us) struggle with. Don't panic if you see yourself in these examples. Remember, this isn't about guilt; it's about growth.

Identifying Controlling Tendencies

Control can wear a lot of different outfits. It might look like telling your partner what they should wear, needing constant updates on their whereabouts, or getting frustrated when a friend doesn't text back fast enough. It might feel like "just caring" or "looking out for someone," but it can also signal a deeper fear of uncertainty or loss.

Control can also show up as manipulation—using guilt, silent treatment, or subtle pressure to get your way. Maybe you've caught yourself saying things like, "I guess I just care more than you do," when what you really mean is, "I'm scared I'm not being chosen."

According to a 2022 study published in the *Journal of Social and Personal Relationships*, controlling behaviors—especially those masked as concern—are among the top predictors of emotional distance and eventual breakups (Apostolou, 2022). The good news? Once you're aware of this tendency, you can begin choosing trust over control. And trust, as we'll explore more in this book, is the oxygen of healthy relationships.

Recognizing Constant Criticism

Criticism can be sneaky. It can come out as sarcasm, back-handed compliments, or even "helpful suggestions" that chip away at someone's self-worth. Maybe you've heard yourself say things like, "Are you really going to wear that?" or "Why can't you ever do things right the first time?"

Here's the thing: There's a big difference between giving feedback and constantly finding fault. Regular criticism—especially about things that don't truly matter—can push people away, damage their confidence, and breed resentment.

Psychologist John Gottman, known for predicting divorce with startling accuracy, calls criticism one of the "four horsemen of the apocalypse" in relationships (Lisitsa, 2024). Why? Because it doesn't just address behavior; it attacks character. Becoming aware of this pattern doesn't mean you stop being honest. It means you learn to speak with kindness and curiosity instead of judgment.

Understanding Emotional Volatility

Have you ever had a reaction that felt way bigger than the moment? Maybe you snapped during a minor disagreement, shut down for hours, or cried out of nowhere and didn't know why. That's emotional volatility. And while we all have ups and downs, consistent emotional explosions or total shutdowns can make the people around us feel like they're walking on eggshells.

That was Harry, though he wouldn't have called it that back then.

In his first marriage, Harry didn't raise his voice much. But he'd get quiet, cold, and distant when something didn't go as he thought it should. He'd stew in silence, thinking he was being "calm" while his wife wrestled with the emotional weight of his withdrawal. If she brought something up that felt like criticism, even something small, like asking for more help with the kids or expressing that she felt unappreciated, he'd shut down for hours, sometimes days.

Harry didn't realize until much later that he wasn't just avoiding conflict. He was avoiding discomfort, and under that discomfort was fear. Fear of not being good enough, fear of losing control, fear of not being needed in the way he was raised to believe he should be.

Unchecked emotional responses often stem from unprocessed wounds or unmet needs. They can create a relational pattern where others stop sharing how they feel, not because they don't care, but because they're afraid of the fallout.

For Harry, therapy helped him realize that his emotional shutdowns weren't protecting his relationship; they were slowly eroding it. Learning his emotional triggers didn't mean silencing his feelings. It meant learning to recognize when a conversation was activating something deeper, so he could pause, breathe, and respond rather than retreat or explode.

It's not uncommon to lose control of our emotions in close relationships. You're not alone, and you're not broken. You're just ready to explore what's underneath. And that's powerful.

Acknowledging Self-Absorption

In the age of selfies and constant scrolling, it's easy to slip into self-centered habits. But in relationships, when conversations always revolve around your day, your stress, and your dreams, it can leave the other person feeling invisible.

Self-absorption doesn't always look like arrogance. Sometimes, it looks like being stuck in your own head. Forgetting to ask, "How are you, really?" or mentally checking out when someone else is sharing. But connection thrives on curiosity. It needs give and take.

Harry didn't see himself as self-absorbed. He provided for his family, and he worked long hours. He believed he was doing everything right. But when his wife tried to open up about feeling overwhelmed or lonely, Harry often redirected the conversation, usually back to his own stress, or brushed it off entirely. He didn't mean to be dismissive. He thought he was being efficient. Solution-focused. "Just tell me what you need, and I'll fix it," he'd say.

But sometimes people don't want a fix. They want a witness.

Harry never realized how little space he was leaving for his wife's inner world until he found himself with someone new. Engaged again, yes—but also determined not to repeat his mistakes. This time, he started asking more questions, listening with intent, and sharing emotional space. This wasn't comfortable for him in the beginning. Vulnerability isn't always easy, but for Harry, it was worth it.

Interestingly, research from the University of California found that couples who share emotional space equally—both speaking and listening—report 33% higher relationship satisfaction (Walker et al., 2023). Just being more present and interested in someone else's world can change everything.

Recognizing toxic behaviors in yourself isn't easy. It takes guts, compassion, and a willingness to evolve. But this is your mirror.

Your moment to see yourself more clearly—not to judge, but to grow. Because when you can spot these patterns, you can change them. And when you change them, you make space for the kind of love, connection, and peace that grows.

Understand the Impact of Toxic Patterns on Relationships

Toxic behaviors aren't just momentary missteps; they ripple through every corner of a relationship, often quietly at first, then loudly, leaving behind confusion, hurt, and emotional distance. When left unchecked, these patterns don't just strain the connection between two people—they unravel it.

Understanding how these behaviors affect your relationships shouldn't center around pointing fingers or drowning in guilt. Instead, focus on recognizing the cost of staying stuck and choose something better. Let's look at the major ways toxic behaviors impact your connections, with real-life moments you might recognize in your own story.

Deterioration of Trust

Trust is the invisible thread that holds relationships together. Once it begins to fray, everything else starts to feel fragile. Toxic behaviors like lying, withholding information, controlling others, or constantly criticizing can chip away at trust little by little.

Take Emma, for example. She often checked her partner's

phone without telling him, convinced it was "just to feel secure." Over time, he stopped sharing details about his day, not out of secrecy, but exhaustion. He didn't feel safe. And she didn't feel closer, only more anxious.

Trust, once damaged, takes time and consistency to rebuild. But when you recognize that your behavior may be contributing to its erosion, you can also be the one to start repairing it. A 2021 survey by *Psychology Today* reported that trust was the number one quality people valued most in long-term relationships and the hardest one to regain once broken (Gunther, 2021).

Building awareness here doesn't mean you've failed. It means you're ready to take responsibility for how you show up, and that's powerful.

Creating Emotional Distance

You can sleep in the same bed and still feel miles apart. Toxic patterns, like shutting down during arguments, using sarcasm instead of honesty, or emotionally exploding over small issues, create an environment where vulnerability feels unsafe. And when that happens, emotional walls go up.

Think of it like this: Every time someone feels invalidated, dismissed, or attacked, they take one step back. Eventually, you're on opposite sides of the room—still together, but no longer connected.

Rosa and Marcus used to talk for hours. Lately, conversations felt transactional—"Did you pay the bill?" "What time's the pickup?"—because emotional connection had quietly slipped away, buried under years of criticism and unresolved tension.

Recognizing how your words, tone, or silence impact closeness, you can fix it. When you become more aware of what builds connection and what breaks it, you start showing up with intention, not just reaction.

The Cycle of Conflict

One argument doesn't break a relationship. But the same argument, on repeat, absolutely can.

Toxic behaviors often create looping patterns. Fights that never get resolved because the root issue isn't addressed. It's not just what you're fighting about, but how you're fighting. Are you blaming? Stonewalling? Getting defensive every time feedback is offered?

Take Sam and Jess. Every disagreement escalated fast. Sam would yell. Jess would shut down. Neither felt heard, both felt hurt. And nothing ever really changed.

The truth is, conflict isn't the enemy. In fact, healthy conflict can lead to deeper understanding. But toxic conflict? That's like putting a Band-Aid on a broken pipe. It might stop the flow for a moment, but eventually, the damage is pouring out everywhere.

By recognizing these cycles, you can stop reacting and start responding. You can ask, "What's really going on underneath this?" And that question alone can shift everything.

Impacts on Self-Esteem

Your relationships are mirrors. When they're loving and respectful, they reflect your worth back to you. But in toxic dynamics—especially ones filled with criticism, control, or manipulation—those mirrors can distort your reflection.

Over time, you might start believing things like:

· *I'm too sensitive.*
· *I always mess things up.*
· *Maybe I am hard to love.*

That's not truth; it's internalized pain. And the longer you stay in relationships where toxic behaviors go unchecked (especially your own), the harder it becomes to separate your identity from the dysfunction.

But here's the shift: When you recognize how your behavior might be hurting someone else's self-esteem—or your own—you can make new choices. You can communicate differently. Listen more. Criticize less. Apologize without conditions. All of this helps rebuild not only connection but also confidence.

Identify Personal Triggers Contributing to Behavior

Have you ever found yourself snapping at someone and wondering, *Where did that come from?* You're not alone. Toxic behaviors don't just appear out of thin air; they usually stem from personal triggers that ignite them like emotional landmines. The key to change isn't just managing the behavior after it explodes, but understanding what sets it off in the first place.

This part of the journey is all about going inward with curiosity, not criticism. When you get honest about what's really bothering you, you reclaim the power to respond instead of react. Let's explore common categories of triggers and how they quietly shape the way we act in relationships.

Recognizing Environmental Triggers

Sometimes, it's not who you're with, but where you are or what you're handling that lights the emotional fuse. Environmental triggers are those external stressors—chaotic mornings, public pressure, financial strain, or even overstimulation—that push you into survival mode.

For example, imagine it's Monday morning. You're already running late, your phone won't stop buzzing, and then your partner asks if you remembered to pay the electric bill. You snap—not because of the question, but because your nervous system is already fried.

Becoming aware of your environmental triggers—like loud spaces, too many demands, or lack of sleep—helps you create more buffer between stress and reaction. It allows you to say, "I'm overstimulated right now. I need a moment." That moment can make all the difference.

Exploring Relationship Dynamics

Certain relationship dynamics can also act as emotional pressure cookers. Ever noticed how you can be calm with some people, but reactive with others? That's not a coincidence. It's often tied to power imbalances, unspoken resentment, or unresolved tension.

Let's say you have a friend who constantly interrupts you. You try to stay calm, but eventually, you lash out or go cold. It's not just the interruption; it's what it represents to you. Maybe it reminds you of not feeling heard as a kid, or being overlooked at work.

When you identify patterns in specific relationships that provoke your toxic responses—like people-pleasing with your boss, or passive-aggression with your partner—you begin to understand the dynamic, not just the outburst. And that understanding can lead to healthier boundaries, clearer communication, and more compassion for them and for yourself.

Self-Reflection on Past Experiences

Many of our most intense reactions are echoes of old pain. That defensive comment? Maybe it's not just about the present disagreement; it's a reflex you developed from growing up in a home where you had to defend yourself constantly. That need to control? Maybe it's rooted in a time when everything felt unpredictable and unsafe.

Chelsea, for instance, realized she kept accusing her partner of pulling away emotionally—not because he was, but because her father left when she was eight, and every delay in a text felt like abandonment all over again.

Reflecting on past experiences doesn't mean you need to stay stuck there. Instead, focus on connecting the dots. When you know your history, you can start writing a new story—one where fear doesn't get the last word.

Identifying Emotional Responses

Now, let's focus on the emotional storm itself. Recognizing what you're feeling when a toxic behavior erupts is crucial. Is it embarrassment that makes you lash out? Is it fear that fuels your need to control? Is it jealousy that leads to passive-aggressive comments?

Think of emotions like a dashboard—they're giving you necessary signals. The problem comes when we ignore those signals and just hit the gas. Naming your emotions ("I'm feeling rejected," "I'm scared," "I'm hurt") doesn't make you weak; it makes you wise. It creates space between the feeling and the behavior, giving you the opportunity to choose a healthier response.

One simple but powerful practice? When you feel triggered, pause and ask yourself: *What am I feeling? Where is this really coming from?* That moment of inquiry might just save you from saying something you can't unsay.

Use Self-Reflection Exercises for Awareness

Awareness is the doorway to change, and self-reflection is the key that unlocks it.

Recognizing toxic patterns isn't a one-time "aha" moment. It's a continuous practice of checking in with yourself, asking the hard questions, and staying open to what you find. Self-reflection doesn't have to be complicated or overwhelming. In fact, it can be incredibly grounding and even liberating, especially when you start noticing small shifts in how you show up for yourself and others.

Let's explore powerful self-reflection tools you can start using right now to build awareness, shift patterns, and create more intentional, connected relationships.

Journaling Prompts

When you put pen to paper, patterns start to emerge. You begin to see the "why" behind your reactions and the emotions that drive your behaviors. Journaling creates space for honesty without judgment, and that's where growth happens.

Try these prompts:

- *What situations tend to trigger my strongest emotional reactions?*
- *When do I feel the most out of control in my relationships, and what usually leads up to it?*
- *What toxic behavior have I used to protect myself? What am I truly afraid of underneath it?*
- *If I could speak to the version of me who reacted poorly, what would I say with compassion?*

The beauty of journaling is that it's both a release and a record. Over time, you can look back and trace your growth. You'll see how your insights deepen, your patterns shift, and your self-awareness expands.

Mindfulness Practices

Mindfulness is about learning to observe your thoughts and feelings without immediately reacting to them. It's like watching a storm pass by instead of getting swept up in it. When practiced regularly, mindfulness helps you hit pause before responding, giving you a chance to choose how you show up.

Try this simple daily exercise:

- **One-minute check-in:** Sit still, close your eyes, and ask yourself, *What's happening in my body? What's on my mind? What emotion is here right now?* No fixing, just noticing.

Even five minutes of mindful breathing, body scanning, or emotional labeling can change your brain's default settings. Studies show that consistent mindfulness practice increases activity in the prefrontal cortex, your center for decision-making and emotional regulation (Verma et al., 2022).

More calm equals less reactivity. More awareness equals more compassionate choices.

Feedback From Trusted Individuals

Sometimes, others see our blind spots before we do. That's why asking for feedback from someone you trust and who cares about your growth can be incredibly valuable. It's not always easy, but it can lead to powerful insights and breakthroughs.

Try starting the conversation with these prompts:

- "I've been working on becoming more self-aware. Have you noticed any patterns in how I show up, especially during conflict?"
- "Is there anything I do that you think might unintentionally

hurt or distance people?"

The key here is choosing someone who's honest but kind—someone who can offer feedback that's meant to help, not harm. And when they speak, try listening without defending. Just breathe, take it in, and let it guide your next steps.

When you acknowledge the insights of others, you create accountability. And that's a major step in transforming your relationships from reactive to reflective.

Behavioral Tracking

If you've ever kept a food diary, budget spreadsheet, or step counter, you already know the power of tracking. The same principle applies to your behavior. When you start documenting emotional triggers, reactions, and patterns, you begin to spot what's happening *before* things spiral.

Here's how to try it:

- Use a journal, app, or notes on your phone.
- Track situations where you felt triggered, how you responded, and how you felt afterward.
- Make notes on what you wish you had done differently or what went well.

You might notice patterns like:

- "I get irritable when I haven't eaten or slept enough."

· "I shut down whenever I feel criticized."
· "I handled that disagreement better after taking a few breaths first."

Tracking not only reveals your toxic patterns; it also shows your progress. And celebrating those small wins builds momentum. You start realizing: *I'm not who I used to be. I'm growing.*

Final Thoughts: You're Not Broken—You're Becoming Aware

I want you to take a moment to appreciate your bravery. Seriously. Looking inward isn't easy. It takes guts to examine your patterns, name your triggers, and admit where things might've gone sideways. But you're doing it, and that means something is already shifting.

Keep going. Keep journaling. Keep pausing when your emotions flare. Keep asking for feedback, not because you're flawed, but because you're growing. That's what this process is about.

And now that you're becoming more aware of your behavior, it's time to zoom out and look at why you may relate the way you do in the first place: Why you cling. Why you avoid. Why you pull people close, only to push them away.

In the next chapter, we're diving into attachment styles—those early emotional blueprints that shape the way we connect, love, and protect ourselves. Spoiler alert: This will connect so many dots for you.

Ready to meet your inner relationship map? Let's turn the page.

2

Understanding Attachment Styles

Carrie was the queen of first dates. Funny, smart, stylish, and genuinely kind, she never had a problem getting attention. But keeping a relationship from crashing into flames within a few weeks? That was another story.

Her last breakup had been the final straw. "Too much," the guy had said. "You're amazing, but so unpredictable."

Carrie was devastated, but also, deep down, a little curious. Why did she go from cool and confident to a full-blown panic attack after a delayed text message? Why did she re-read old messages like they were sacred texts, or convince herself she was being ghosted after one slow reply? And, um, why did she once send 52 texts in a 24-hour period asking, "Why don't you love me anymore?" (Yep. 52.)

That breakup didn't just leave her broken; it woke her up.

So, she did something radical: She stopped chasing love and

started chasing healing.

In therapy, she discovered a term that made everything click: anxious attachment style. This was more than a label; it was a mirror. Suddenly, her spirals made sense. So did her tendency to cling too tightly, fear abandonment, and seek constant reassurance.

Most of us walk into relationships carrying invisible blueprints we didn't even know we were following. These patterns are called attachment styles. They're behind our reactions, our triggers, and our relationship habits, good and toxic.

In this chapter, we're going to unpack the four main attachment styles:

- **Secure attachment:** the ideal, but not the only goal
- **Anxious attachment:** Carrie's crew
- **Avoidant attachment:** the emotionally elusive
- **Disorganized attachment:** the push-pull roller coaster

You'll discover how each style shows up in everyday behavior—texting habits, arguments, intimacy issues, and more. We'll explore how your past shaped your current patterns, and most importantly, how to shift them.

Whether you're currently in a relationship, healing from a toxic one, or just ready to understand yourself better, this chapter will give you the insight and tools to start showing up differently, compassionately, mindfully. And with more emotional clarity than ever before.

It's time to rewrite the pattern, and it starts right here.

Assessing Your Attachment Style Through Quizzes

Before Carrie started her healing journey, she thought she was just bad at love. Too clingy. Too intense. Too quick to spiral. But the moment she took an attachment quiz and saw the words anxious-preoccupied pop up, it was like someone had finally handed her a map. Suddenly, the emotional whiplash, the overthinking, the need for constant reassurance—it all made sense.

You can get that same clarity right now.

The Purpose of Attachment Quizzes

Attachment quizzes aren't personality tests for entertainment; they're self-awareness tools. They help you spot the patterns in your relationship behavior:

- How do you respond to closeness and distance?
- How do you cope with emotional triggers?
- How has your childhood shaped your current wiring?

Workbook Activity: Discover Your Attachment Style

Read each question and choose the answer that feels most true for you in romantic or emotionally close relationships. Circle or highlight your answers.

When your partner pulls away or goes quiet, how do you usually feel?

A. Panicked or worried: I might overanalyze or reach out repeatedly.

B. Relieved: I need space, too.

C. Confused: I want closeness but also feel uncomfortable with it.

D. Calm: I trust they'll come back and we'll reconnect.

How do you typically respond during a disagreement?

A. I get anxious, afraid they'll leave or stop loving me.

B. I shut down or avoid the conversation altogether.

C. I flip-flop. Sometimes, I fight hard; sometimes, I shut down.

D. I can express myself clearly and also listen to them.

When things are going well, do you ever feel... suspicious?

A. Yes, I often worry it's "too good to be true."

B. Not really—I try not to get too attached.

C. Sometimes. I want to trust, but my guard stays up.

D. No, I feel safe and secure in good moments.

How do you feel about emotional intimacy?

A. I crave it and sometimes overdo it.

B. It makes me a little uncomfortable. I prefer independence.

C. I want it badly, but I fear I'll get hurt.

D. I enjoy it and find it helps relationships grow stronger.

How do you typically feel when you're alone or single?

A. Lonely or restless: I want connection fast.

B. Totally fine, maybe even better than when I'm with some-one.

C. Torn: I want love, but I'm afraid of it.

D. Peaceful: I use the time to grow and enjoy life.

Tally Up Your Answers

Count how many A's, B's, C's, and D's you chose:

- A: _____
- B: _____
- C: _____
- D: _____

What Your Results Suggest

Mostly A's—Anxious attachment: You may worry about being abandoned, seek frequent reassurance, and fear disconnection. You care deeply and love hard—your work is learning to self-soothe and build trust from the inside out.

Mostly B's—Avoidant attachment: You value independence and may struggle with too much closeness. You're likely strong and resourceful, and your next step is allowing emotional intimacy to feel safe, not threatening.

Mostly C's—Disorganized attachment: You may crave love and connection but fear it at the same time. Your experiences may have left you unsure whether intimacy brings safety or pain. Healing past wounds and rebuilding trust is key.

Mostly D's—Secure attachment: You feel confident giving and receiving love. You can set boundaries, express needs, and handle conflict without losing yourself. This is the foundation of healthy, balanced relationships—and something we all can work toward.

Now, Let's Reflect

Reflection questions (write in the space offered):

- How does your attachment style show up in your current or past relationships?
- What specific situations trigger your strongest emotional reactions?
- How has your upbringing or past experience shaped this style?
- What kind of relationships do you want to create moving forward?
- What's one small, powerful shift you can make starting today?

Journaling Prompt

What has my attachment style taught me about how I protect myself, and how do I want to love differently moving forward?

Write freely. There's no wrong answer. This is about insight, not perfection.

Your attachment style is not your identity. It's just a pattern, and every pattern can be unlearned, reshaped, and healed.

Learning About the Secure Attachment Style

Let's talk about the gold standard of attachment styles: secure attachment. Now, if that phrase makes you picture someone who meditates daily, journals about their feelings, and never freaks out over a delayed text, don't worry. Secure attachment doesn't mean you're perfect or emotionless. It simply means you feel safe being yourself in a relationship, and you trust others to meet you there.

Sound dreamy? That's because it kind of is. But here's the twist: It's not just for people who had picture-perfect childhoods or superhuman emotional control. It's something you can learn, grow into, and practice—at any point in your life.

Let's break it down.

What Is Secure Attachment?

People with secure attachment tend to

- feel confident and grounded in their relationships.
- communicate needs honestly without fear or guilt.

- handle emotional ups and downs without spiraling.
- trust others, and themselves, to weather hard moments together.

They're not immune to hurt, but they don't assume every bump means a breakup. They don't chase or run. They pause, process, and respond with curiosity.

In short, secure individuals know they're lovable, and they believe others are, too.

Why Secure Attachment Is So Powerful

Secure attachment isn't just good for you—it transforms the entire relationship dynamic. Here's why:

- People with secure attachment handle conflict with resilience. They can disagree without going into attack, retreat, or people-please mode.
- They encourage emotional openness. Instead of shutting down or freaking out, they lean in. They ask, "Tell me what you need."
- They balance closeness and independence. Secure people don't lose themselves in love, and they don't fear being close. They make space for you while honoring space for themselves.

Whether it's a romantic partner, a best friend, or a family member—secure attachment lays the foundation for safe, honest, and deeply satisfying connection.

How to Cultivate Secure Attachment

Spoiler alert: You don't need a time machine to rewrite your childhood. You just need courage, consistency, and compassion.

Here's how to start building secure attachment—right now:

- **Practice self-awareness:** Notice your emotional triggers without judging them. Observe your reactions with curiosity: *Why did that text make me panic?*
- **Seek support:** A good therapist, coach, or even secure friend can model healthy attachment and help rewire your patterns.
- **Reflect on past dynamics:** Identify old relationship behaviors that no longer serve you. Then gently ask yourself: *What would a secure response look like?*
- **Build self-trust:** Every time you soothe your own anxiety, set a boundary, or speak your truth, you are reinforcing that you've got your own back. That's how secure attachment begins.

Real-Life Examples: What Secure Attachment Looks Like

Let's say two people—Jordan and Maya—are in a relationship. One night, Jordan is quiet and withdrawn. Instead of assuming the worst, Maya asks gently, "You seem off. Want to talk about it?" Jordan opens up about a rough day at work. They talk, reconnect, and move forward—no passive-aggressive jabs, no silent treatments, no emotional rollercoasters.

This is secure attachment in action: Honest. Safe. Human.

Or take Serena, who used to have an anxious style but began doing the work. She started pausing before reacting, checking in with her body, and reminding herself that she is safe—even if someone takes a little longer to respond. Her relationships became calmer, her confidence grew, and her inner world started to feel like home.

These aren't just "healthy people" stories; they're *your* stories in the making.

Exploring Anxious Attachment Style Traits

Let's bring Carrie back. Remember her 52-text moment of doom? That moment didn't come out of nowhere. It came from an attachment style that had been quietly shaping her love life like a behind-the-scenes director yelling, "Don't trust this! Text again! Maybe one more! Okay, now panic!"

After a string of relationships that went from red-hot to red-flag real quick, Carrie realized something powerful: It wasn't just them. It was how she attached.

If you've ever felt like your emotions were "too much" or worried someone pulling away meant the relationship was ending, welcome to the anxious club (no membership card, but lots of emotional spirals).

Common traits include:

- **Fear of abandonment:** A late reply can feel like a breakup announcement.
- **Clinginess:** Not because you're needy, but because love feels safest when you're *really* close.
- **Constant need for reassurance:** You might ask, "Are we okay?" even if things seem fine.
- **Overthinking every interaction:** What did they mean by "ok"? WHY DIDN'T THEY USE A HEART EMOJI??

These aren't flaws, they're survival responses. Often rooted in inconsistent caregiving during childhood, they can leave you emotionally wired for rejection.

How Anxious Attachment Impacts Relationships

Carrie's relationships were like emotional rollercoasters—thrilling in the beginning, but exhausting after a few weeks. She craved constant reassurance and overanalyzed everything. One partner said, "I feel like I can't breathe without triggering a meltdown."

That hit hard. But it also became her wake-up call.

Here's what often happens:

- Anxious partners may unintentionally overwhelm others with their emotional needs.
- Tension rises when every pause or change feels like a threat.

· Otherwise healthy relationships get strained because minor issues feel catastrophic.

The intention is love and closeness. But the impact? Often the opposite.

How Carrie Started Healing Her Anxious Attachment

Carrie knew she couldn't keep spiraling with every unread message. She started doing the work:

· She learned to self-soothe. Deep breathing, journaling, and talking to her inner child helped her calm her racing thoughts before reacting.
· She got real with her partners. "Hey, I sometimes feel panicky when I don't hear from you, and I'm working on it. Can we talk about it together?"
· She practiced mindfulness. Instead of jumping to conclusions, she grounded herself in the present: *What do I know to be true right now?*

It didn't happen overnight. But slowly, she moved from fear to trust. From chasing love to creating it.

Case Study: Carrie, Rewritten

A year later, Carrie was in a new relationship—and this time, it looked different. When her partner went quiet after a stressful day at work, she didn't panic. She gave him space and checked in with herself first. Then she sent a single message: "Thinking of you. Let me know when you're up for talking."

He replied two hours later with, "Rough day. I'm so grateful you're patient with me."

That's what healing looks like.

Identifying the Avoidant Attachment Style

If anxious attachment is a scream for connection, avoidant attachment is a whisper that says, *I'm fine without anyone.*

Avoidantly attached individuals are often proud of their self-sufficiency. They downplay emotional needs—not because they don't have them, but because they've learned not to trust others to meet them.

Characteristics of Avoidant Attachment

Let's break down what this style looks like in action:

- **High value on independence:** "I don't *need* anyone."
- **Emotional distance:** Feelings make them uneasy.
- **Downplaying the importance of relationships:** "I'm just better off alone."
- **Struggling with vulnerability:** Sharing feelings feels risky and uncomfortable.

Avoidant individuals often had caregivers who were emotionally unavailable or dismissive. The unspoken lesson? Don't rely on anyone.

Impact on Relationships

Here's what often happens in avoidant partnerships:

- They keep others at arm's length.
- Emotional conversations feel threatening or exhausting.
- Partners may feel unimportant, invisible, or starved for connection.

It's not about being cold—it's about safety. But walls don't just keep others out. They keep you in, too.

Strategies for Avoidant Individuals

The good news? Avoidant attachment is not a life sentence. Healing begins with small, intentional steps:

- Practice vulnerability in safe, low-stakes moments. "I felt overwhelmed today" is a great start.
- Name your needs. Not with a bullhorn—just a whisper. "I need some space, but I care about us."
- Work with a therapist. Emotional connection may feel foreign, but with the right support, you can learn a new language of intimacy.

Real-Life Reflections

Take Marcus, for example. He used to freeze when his girlfriend cried. It felt like pressure. Like failure. But with time, he learned to sit beside her, hold her hand, and simply say, "I'm here."

His fear of being consumed by someone else's emotions began to shift. He didn't have to solve it—just be present. And that presence changed everything.

Understanding Disorganized Attachment

Some people want to get close... and also want to run away. They crave intimacy, but panic when they get it. They fear abandonment, but also fear being truly seen.

If this sounds like a tug-of-war in your chest, you might relate to disorganized attachment.

This style is often the most complex because it's rooted in early relationships that were both a source of love *and* fear. Inconsistent, neglectful, abusive, or traumatic caregiving in childhood can create a deep internal confusion: *Can I trust you? Or will you hurt me?*

Characteristics of Disorganized Attachment

Disorganized attachment is sometimes called "fearful-avoidant," and for good reason. People with this style might:

- Desire connection but fear intimacy at the same time.
- Struggle with self-worth, feeling unlovable or damaged.
- Swing between anxious and avoidant behaviors—clingy one moment, distant the next.
- Have intense reactions to conflict or perceived rejection.
- Sabotage healthy relationships because they feel too foreign or unsafe.

Imagine driving with one foot on the gas and one on the brake. That's what disorganized attachment can feel like emotionally—exhausting, confusing, and hard to explain to others (or even to yourself).

Impact on Relationships

Disorganized attachment can create a storm of contradictions in relationships:

- You might feel desperate for love and terrified of it.
- You might test people's loyalty, then push them away.
- You might replay childhood trauma through adult dynamics, even when you know they're unhealthy.

This was Carrie's deepest layer. At first, she thought she

was just anxious. But through deeper therapy work, she uncovered early emotional chaos that shaped her idea of love as unpredictable and dangerous. Her partners weren't just pulling away—she was, too, in her own way. Her fear of being hurt made her cling, lash out, withdraw, and collapse in shame—all in the same relationship.

Once she saw this, everything started to shift.

Strategies for Healing Disorganized Attachment

Healing from disorganized attachment takes patience, compassion, and often professional support. But it *is* possible. Many people with this style go on to form beautifully secure relationships after doing the work.

Here's where to begin:

- **Acknowledge the paradox:** It's okay to both want love and fear it. That awareness is powerful.
- **Create emotional safety:** Healing begins when you feel safe with yourself. Use grounding, breathwork, and inner child work to nurture your nervous system.
- **Work with a trauma-informed therapist:** EMDR, IFS, and somatic therapy can be transformative for healing early attachment wounds.
- **Practice co-regulation:** Let someone *safe* in. Slowly. Share your fears. Let them prove they're not your past.
- **Celebrate progress:** Even pausing before reacting is a win. Reaching out instead of shutting down is healing. You're

re–patterning one moment at a time.

Real-World Insight: The New Carrie

As Carrie began healing her deeper wounds, she stopped blaming herself for being "too much" or "not enough." She started naming her triggers, regulating her responses, and building safer connections. The anxiety didn't disappear overnight, but her fear no longer ran the show.

One day, her partner forgot a dinner plan. In the past, she would've spiraled—crying, texting, detaching. But this time, she paused. Took a breath. Then said, "That hurt, but I know you didn't mean to disappoint me. Can we talk about it?"

That wasn't just a win. That was transformation.

Final Thoughts: From Understanding to Empowerment

By now, you've taken a brave step: You've looked inward. You've explored the ways your past has shaped how you love, how you fear, and how you respond when things feel uncertain. You've walked alongside Carrie, felt her panic, her growth, her breakthrough, and maybe even seen parts of yourself in her story.

The fact that you're reading this means you're already in motion. You're unlearning what hurt you, and you're stepping into awareness.

So... what comes next?

Now that you understand why your nervous system may panic over a missed call or why silence makes your brain write dramatic breakup scripts, it's time to learn how to quiet the storm inside.

In the next chapter, we'll dive into practical, science-backed techniques for managing anxiety and overthinking in relationships. This is where knowledge becomes action. Where awareness becomes change, and where you learn to hold yourself with the kind of love and stability you've always deserved.

3

Managing Anxiety and Overthinking

James, 43, spent most of his life performing a version of manhood that wasn't truly his. Growing up as the youngest of four rough-and-tumble brothers—and the son of a tough, no-excuses military father—he was taught that emotions were a liability. Sensitivity wasn't just frowned upon; it was crushed under teasing, eye rolls, and dismissive jokes.

"Man up."

"Stop crying."

"Get it together."

Those messages didn't just shape him—they *hardened* him.

By the time James became a husband, a father, and a successful accountant, he wore his armor well. On the outside, he was sarcastic, efficient, controlled. Inside, though, he was unraveling. He desperately craved intimacy—the kind of deep, emotional connection that makes a relationship feel like home—but he had no idea how to create it without feeling exposed and "weak."

Toxic patterns had taken root without him even realizing it:

- **Dismissiveness:** brushing off his wife's emotions with jokes or sarcasm
- **Control:** constantly needing reassurance, but disguising it through criticism or withdrawal
- **Emotional shutdowns:** retreating into work or silence when he felt overwhelmed

These behaviors slowly built walls between him and the very people he loved most. Deep down, James felt lonely. Misunderstood. Frustrated that no matter how much he wanted closeness, it always seemed just out of reach.

When anxiety and overthinking eventually led him to therapy, he was given tools like journaling and grounding exercises, but using them felt wrong. Foreign. Vulnerable. Too not him.

When he finally mustered the courage to open up to his brothers, hoping for a shred of support, their teasing cut deep.

"You need a bubble bath or something?" they joked. James laughed along, but inside, he shrank.

The Shift: Choosing a New Way Forward

It wasn't a lecture, a book, or a therapy worksheet that finally opened the door to change—it was something much quieter.

On long walks by the lake, casting his fishing line into still water, lying in the backyard watching clouds roll across the sky, James found something he'd never been given permission to explore: stillness. Space. Gentleness.

Without even knowing it, James had stumbled into mindfulness. It didn't feel like weakness. It didn't feel like therapy. It felt like freedom.

Here's what we're going to explore together in this chapter:

- why pressure to "toughen up" can lead to toxic behaviors
- how anxiety and overthinking take root in relationships
- what healing looks like—not just in theory, but in real life
- doable, grounded techniques to calm your nervous system and reconnect with yourself
- how to communicate your fears in ways that strengthen (not sabotage) your relationships
- how to heal after a breakup when your mind keeps replaying old patterns

You deserve relationships where you feel safe, loved, and deeply connected. Let's start by healing the habits that hold you back— and building something real, honest, and lasting.

Practice Grounding Techniques Daily

Anxious thoughts love the future. They sprint ahead:

- *What if she's mad?*
- *What if she leaves?*
- *What if I mess it all up again?*

For James, this kind of thinking used to take over his entire day. A missed text could spiral into panic. A quiet dinner could launch a hundred worst-case scenarios in his mind.

He didn't realize it yet, but what he desperately needed was an anchor—something to pull him out of the swirling "what-ifs" and back into the safety of the present moment.

Grounding is your way of saying: *Not now, brain. We're here. We're safe.*

According to research, consistent use of grounding techniques can reduce emotional overwhelm and improve emotional regulation in people with anxiety and trauma histories (Nakao et al., 2021). Simply put: The more you practice staying present, the easier it becomes to stop overthinking before it spirals out of control.

Understanding Grounding: Why It Works

Anxiety tricks us into believing disaster is happening right now—even when it's not. This imagined crisis activates your stress response, flooding your body with cortisol and cutting you off from logic, compassion, and connection.

For James, it meant snapping at his wife over tiny misunderstandings. Withdrawing when he needed closeness most. Feeling like he had to manage and control every little thing to "stay safe."

Grounding pulls you out of that loop. It shifts your focus from fear of the future to awareness of the now. When you're grounded, you're not stuck in past regrets or future fears— you're here. And *here* is where healing happens.

For James, grounding didn't start in a therapist's office. It started on a cool morning when he noticed the crisp air on his face during a sunrise hike. It started while listening to the ripples of the lake while fishing. It started when he paused long enough to feel—really feel—the world around him.

That stillness was his first real breath of peace.

Try This: The 5-4-3-2-1 Technique

This popular grounding exercise uses your senses to interrupt anxious thinking:

- 5 things you can *see*
- 4 things you can *touch*
- 3 things you can *hear*
- 2 things you can *smell*
- 1 thing you can *taste*

This simple technique calms the nervous system and brings attention away from racing thoughts. It's discreet, portable, and can be done anywhere. You can do it on the bus, in your office, or even in the middle of a tough conversation.

You can also do this:

- Carry a grounding object in your pocket (a smooth stone, a marble, or magnetic rocks).
- Walk barefoot on grass or carpet.
- Drink cold water slowly and mindfully.
- Play a game like "Name that Color" or "Count the Rectangles in the Room" to redirect your focus.

The best grounding technique is the one you'll actually use, so choose what fits your vibe.

Creating a Grounding Routine

One of James's biggest shifts came when he stopped treating grounding like an emergency fire extinguisher and started making it a daily habit.

Think of grounding like brushing your teeth. You don't wait

until your teeth hurt; you brush to prevent the pain.

James built grounding into small pockets of his day:

- While making coffee, he named five sounds he could hear.
- On lunch breaks, he placed a hand on his chest to feel his breath.
- Before bed, he watched the clouds outside his window, letting his senses relax him into sleep.

It wasn't perfect. Some days, he forgot. Some days, it didn't feel like it "worked." But the cumulative effect was undeniable. He started feeling calmer without even trying. His default setting became less panic, more presence.

Studies back this up: Developing daily rituals around grounding techniques increases emotional stability and resilience over time (Koniver, 2022).

Overcoming Resistance: When It Feels Weird or Doesn't "Work"

At first, James felt ridiculous. *I'm a grown man counting tree branches like a kindergartener?* he thought.

Resistance is normal. Feeling silly, impatient, or doubtful doesn't mean you're doing it wrong—it means you're practicing something new. Remember: James spent 40+ years being conditioned to push emotions away. Changing that would take patience and repetition, not perfection.

If you skip a day? Okay. If your mind still races sometimes? Okay. The healing is in the showing up.

Daily grounding is about supporting you. It won't erase your anxiety, but it will soften its grip. It will strengthen your ability to stay steady, even when life isn't.

And just like James discovered, the more grounded you become, the more love, trust, and connection you invite into every relationship you build.

Use Mindfulness Tools for Anxiety Relief

For James, anxiety used to be a silent driver in every relationship. He didn't yell, but he shut down. He didn't explode, but he panicked silently. A text left unread? His mind jumped to worst-case scenarios. A disagreement with his wife? He'd replay the conversation for days, trying to figure out what he should have said. He didn't realize it then, but he wasn't in the moment; he was in the land of what-ifs and what-went-wrongs.

That began to change when his therapist introduced him to mindfulness. Not incense-and-sitting-cross-legged mindfulness, but something simpler: learning how to pause. To notice his thoughts instead of drowning in them. To respond instead of react.

What Is Mindfulness in Relationships, Really?

Mindfulness is the practice of being fully present in the moment, without judgment.

In relationships, that looks like this:

- noticing your partner's words without planning your rebuttal
- being aware of how your body reacts when you're upset—tight chest, clenched jaw—and pausing before responding
- catching your anxious thoughts (*She must be mad at me*) and observing them without assuming they're true

Research from Harvard Medical School has shown that mindfulness reduces activity in the brain's "default mode network," the part responsible for rumination and overthinking. The more present we become, the less we spiral (Powell, 2018).

James started small. A breath before answering a tough question. A moment of stillness on the back porch instead of doomscrolling. Surprisingly, these moments helped him feel more in control than all the overthinking ever did.

Mindfulness Practices to Try

Start where you are. Stay with what's real. Let presence do the healing.

Here's the truth: You don't need a meditation cushion, a $200 retreat, or a perfectly quiet mind to begin practicing mindfulness. You just need a moment—and a willingness to notice what's happening, without running from it.

For James, mindfulness wasn't some spiritual awakening. It was survival. After a long pattern of emotional reactivity, detachment, and overwhelm in his relationships, he realized he wasn't just out of sync with others—he was out of sync with himself.

He didn't know what he was feeling until it exploded. He didn't notice tension in his body until it became pain. And he couldn't respond with clarity because his mind was always racing two steps ahead—or stuck five years in the past.

So, he started small:
   Five minutes in the car before picking up his daughter.
   One quiet breath before answering a difficult text.
   A pause at the kitchen sink just to feel his feet on the floor.
   Mindfulness met him exactly where he was—and changed how he related to the world.
   Here are a few of the simple, free, powerful practices James now uses regularly:

Mindful Breathing

"Inhale for four, hold for four, exhale for four."

This basic breath cycle, often called box breathing, is James's

53

go-to when his nervous system starts to rev up. It helps him shift from reactive to responsive, from fight-or-flight to grounded and aware.

Why it works: Your breath is a built-in remote control for your brain. Slow, intentional breathing sends a physiological signal that says: *You're okay. You're safe. You can soften now.*

Try it

- before a tough conversation.
- during a moment of overwhelm.
- lying in bed, when your thoughts won't stop spinning.

Body Scans

"I close my eyes and just check in: Where's the tension? Where's the numbness? What's asking for my attention?"

A body scan is simply taking a few moments to bring awareness to each part of your body—head to toe. Noticing without judging. Feeling without fixing.

James began doing this when he realized he often dissociated during stress—numbing out, disconnecting. The body scan gently brought him back.

Why it works: It anchors you in the present moment. It also helps you recognize where emotion might be living physically (like a clenched jaw or tight shoulders), so you can release it with care.

Try it

- while lying down at night.
- as a reset after a triggering interaction.
- before your morning coffee or after work, to decompress.

Mindful Observation

"I sit outside with no phone. I just watch the sky change. It reminds me the world keeps moving—gently, quietly—even when my mind is loud."

Mindful observation is the art of just *watching*. No judgment. No story. Just being a witness.

Look at the clouds. Watch the breeze move a tree branch. Let your eyes land softly on whatever they see. Resist the urge to label or evaluate. Just let it be.

Why it works: It slows your brain down from its "doing" mode and drops you into "being" mode. It reconnects you with the present and reminds you that presence itself is enough.

Try it

- during a walk.
- in your backyard.
- at a window on a rainy day.

Bonus: One Mindful Minute

Sometimes, one minute of quiet can change the course of your entire day.

You don't need a full session. You need a moment. Mindfulness isn't about time; it's about intention.

James sometimes uses "one mindful minute" before big conversations, when brushing his teeth, or while washing dishes. No distractions. Just breathing and paying attention.

Try it

- before sending a text that feels emotionally loaded.
- while waiting in line.
- before bedtime—just breathing, no scrolling.

Why This Matters in Relationships

James didn't just use mindfulness to feel calmer; he used it to show up differently in love.
　It helped him

- pause before reacting.
- name his feelings instead of acting them out.
- stay emotionally present when others were upset.

· feel safe in his own skin, even when conversations got hard.

Mindfulness made him a better listener, a more grounded parent, and a more emotionally available partner. And it didn't take hours a day—just *practice*.

Practicing Mindfulness in Relationships

Mindfulness doesn't end when you open your eyes—it shows up in how you relate.

Want to be less reactive during a disagreement? Try this:

1. Before responding, pause. Feel your feet on the ground. Take a breath.
2. Notice the urge to "fix" or "defend." Instead, ask yourself: *Can I be curious instead of certain?*
3. Stay aware of your tone, posture, and breath during conversations.

This is what James calls "emotional steering." Instead of letting anxiety drive, he's learning to observe his internal world and choose his next move. That awareness has softened his responses and deepened his connection with his wife and kids.

Implement Thought-Stopping Methods Effectively

James used to fall down mental rabbit holes faster than you could say, "She didn't text back." One small trigger—like his wife seeming distant after work—would snowball into hours of worry. *She's upset. I must have done something. Maybe she's tired of me. Maybe I'm just too much.*

It wasn't just annoying; it was exhausting.

His therapist introduced him to a deceptively simple tool: thought-stopping. The idea? Interrupt the anxious spiral before it takes over. Train your brain to say: "Not today."

Understanding the Thought-Stopping Technique

Thought-stopping is exactly what it sounds like: It's a technique that helps you catch and halt negative, intrusive, or anxious thoughts before they become a full-blown panic cycle.

Instead of fueling the fire, you interrupt it.

This method works by

- breaking the automatic loop of worry.
- shifting your attention from fear to clarity.
- building cognitive control over repetitive thought patterns.

It might feel odd at first, but it's highly effective and empowering.

How to Do It: Step-By-Step

Here's how James started:

1. Catch the thought. *She didn't hug me goodbye this morning. Something's wrong.*
2. Say "STOP." Out loud if possible, or sharply in your mind. Some people even snap a rubber band on their wrist or clap once.
3. Visualize a stop sign or a red light. This creates a powerful mental cue.
4. Replace the thought. Try: *She might be tired. I'll check in with her calmly later.*
5. Refocus your attention. Take a breath. Go for a walk. Do something grounding.

James keeps a sticky note on his desk that says "Catch. Stop. Replace. Refocus." It's his mental emergency brake.

Recognizing Triggers Before They Spiral

Thought-stopping becomes even more powerful when paired with self-awareness. Start by identifying your common anxiety triggers:

- silence from a loved one
- ambiguous text messages
- a disagreement that ended unresolved
- sudden changes in plans

Knowing your triggers helps you prepare for them and apply thought-stopping techniques proactively.

For example, James learned that long gaps in communication triggered childhood wounds around being ignored. Once he knew that, he could meet those moments with tools, not panic.

Replacing Negative Thoughts With Truth and Compassion

Stopping a thought is only part one. Part two is replacing it with something helpful.
Here are two examples:

- Instead of: *She's pulling away,* try: *I don't know what she's feeling, and I can ask without assuming.*
- Instead of: *This always happens,* try: *This moment is new, and I can handle it.*

Positive affirmations focus on reminding yourself of your power to respond differently.

Together, mindfulness and thought-stopping become a powerful combo. One keeps you present. The other keeps you from spiraling. And with time, just like James, you'll find that the anxious noise in your head gets quieter and the clarity in your relationships gets louder.

You're not your thoughts. You're the awareness behind them. And that awareness? That's your superpower.

Apply Breathing Exercises to Calm the Mind

James never thought something as simple as breathing could change his life. For years, he pushed through anxiety with brute force by working late, running errands, or numbing out with noise. ADHD made him feel constantly wired, and anxiety added a relentless undercurrent of worry. His wife would try to talk about their relationship, but he was already in fight-or-flight mode before she finished her second sentence.

During one therapy session, his therapist paused and said, "James, you're not breathing."

And she was right. His chest was tight. His jaw clenched. His shoulders drawn to his ears.

That was the moment James learned that his breath wasn't just automatic—it could be intentional. And intentional breathing changed everything.

Breathing Techniques That Actually Work

Start with one of these simple methods:

Box Breathing (4-4-4-4)

Favored by Navy Seals to stay calm under pressure.

1. Inhale for 4 seconds.
2. Hold for 4 seconds.

3. Exhale for 4 seconds.
4. Hold for 4 seconds.
5. Repeat for 2–5 minutes. Visualize drawing a square with your breath.

4-7-8 Breathing

Ideal for winding down at night or when emotions are running high.

1. Inhale through the nose for 4 seconds.
2. Hold the breath for 7 seconds.
3. Exhale slowly through the mouth for 8 seconds.

This pattern slows the heart rate and resets the nervous system.

Diaphragmatic (Belly) Breathing

Best for ADHD minds that get stuck in shallow, rapid breathing.

1. Place one hand on your chest and the other on your belly.
2. Breathe in through your nose so your belly rises.
3. Exhale slowly so your belly falls.
4. Try to keep the chest as still as possible.

Each of these exercises takes less than five minutes and can be practiced anywhere: your car, the bathroom, during a break at work, or right before bed.

Create a Calm Environment for Maximum Impact

While you can breathe mindfully anywhere, a peaceful setting can amplify the benefits.

James turned his backyard into his personal reset zone. A chair under the trees. No phone. Just wind, breath, and space. He added a small fountain for background sound and made it a ritual—five minutes before leaving for work, five minutes after coming home. It became his way of reclaiming his nervous system before bringing his emotions into his relationships.

Here's how to set the mood:

- Choose a quiet spot—indoor or outdoor—where you won't be interrupted.
- Add calming elements like soft lighting, nature sounds, or scents you love and find calming.
- Pair breathing with something sensory—like holding a warm mug of coffee, or placing a hand over your heart to signal safety to your brain.

These rituals can make breathing exercises something you look forward to, not just something you resort to.

Use Breathing in Real-Life Relationship Moments

Let's talk practicality. You're in the middle of a tense conversation. Your partner says something that triggers defensiveness.

You feel the heat rise in your chest.

This is your cue: pause and breathe. Even just one slow breath can prevent a reactive explosion.

Here are just a few situations where James uses breathing now:

- before answering a tough question from his teen daughter
- when he feels his voice starting to rise in a disagreement
- right after reading a stressful email
- before initiating a vulnerable conversation with his wife

The difference? He no longer bulldozes through his feelings. He breathes through them.

Breathing is the bridge between the mind and body, and it's always available. For men with ADHD and anxiety, breathwork is more than just calming; it's empowering. It brings clarity in chaos, slows down racing thoughts, and allows you to meet your relationships with grounded strength.

So, if your emotions are crashing like waves, remember: You don't need to fight the storm, just anchor your breath. And from that still place, everything else can shift.

Final Thoughts: From Survival Mode to Connection Mode

Throughout this chapter, you've learned how grounding techniques can anchor you, mindfulness can create space between you and your reactions, breath can shift you from chaos to calm in a matter of moments, and thought-stopping can put the brakes on spirals before they take you down.

These aren't just practices. They're lifelines, and when practiced consistently, they reduce anxiety and create the foundation for something deeper: presence.

And presence is everything in relationships. Because when you're present, you can listen without defense. You can speak without fear. You can connect without control.

That's where we're heading next.

In the next chapter, we'll explore effective communication skills—how to speak clearly, listen deeply, and build the kind of trust that anxiety tries to destroy. We'll break down real conversations, decode emotional signals, and offer you a toolkit to communicate not from fear, but from authenticity.

Because when your mind is calm and your words are clear, connection stops being a battlefield and starts becoming a bridge.

Let's cross that bridge together.

4

Effective Communication Skills

Melanie was 36 when she realized her voice wasn't just loud, it was hurting the people she loved most.

Growing up in a home where volume equaled power, Melanie had learned that to be heard, you had to be the loudest in the room. Conflict wasn't something to be resolved; it was something to win. And that mindset followed her like a shadow into every relationship she had. In friendships, she often steamrolled over others without realizing. In parenting, she defaulted to what she called her "mom voice"—the loud one, the one her kids "finally listened to," even though it made her feel horrible after. And in her marriage, she became defensive the moment her husband opened his mouth. She wasn't listening; she was loading ammunition.

Then, came the wake-up call: "If we don't fix this," her husband said quietly, "I can't stay."

Melanie didn't change overnight, but she started therapy. She unpacked the years of emotional survival she'd learned as a kid. She practiced slowing down, breathing through her triggers, and—hardest of all—actually listening. Two years later, their relationship looks completely different. Her voice is still strong, but now it comes with softness, curiosity, and calm.

This chapter is for every Melanie out there—whether you yell, shut down, ghost, over-explain, or go silent when emotions rise. Maybe you're in a relationship right now or picking up the pieces of one that ended? This chapter will help you understand how communication can either build bridges or burn them.

Communication is more than just words. It's how we express love, anger, fear, disappointment, and hope. It's the way we create safety in a relationship, or destroy it. You can learn a better way to speak, connect, and be heard.

Are you ready?

Learn Active Listening Techniques: How to Truly Hear the People You Love—Even When It's Hard

Melanie used to think that listening meant waiting for her turn to speak.

When her husband opened up about something he was struggling with, she was already halfway through crafting her rebuttal. "You don't get it," she'd fire back, raising her voice, cutting him off. "You never listen to me either!" What should have been a moment of connection turned into a battlefield—

each of them tugging hard, neither feeling heard, both left drained.

So, why was this toxic? Instead of creating space for under-standing, Melanie was fueling disconnection. Listening became a bridge. Her automatic need to defend blocked the empathy her relationship desperately needed.

Melanie needed to stop listening to reply and start listening to understand. Through therapy, Melanie discovered a truth that changed everything: real listening isn't about preparing your comeback; it's about laying down your side of the rope and choosing to be present.

She learned active listening techniques—small shifts that made a big difference. And you can too.

Let's dive into how to move from reactive replies to active, healing listening, and how it can radically change your rela-tionships.

Understanding Active Listening

Let's clear something up right away: Active listening is not passive. It's not nodding while mentally drafting a grocery list. It's not waiting for your turn to talk. And it's definitely not about "fixing" the other person.

Active listening is a conscious act of love. It's the decision to stay—fully—with someone's words, their emotion, their moment. It's choosing presence over performance. It's saying with your attention, "You matter. I'm here. I want to understand."

When we actively listen, we're not just hearing the words. We're picking up on:

- **Tone:** Are they angry, hurt, scared, disappointed?
- **Pacing:** Are they rushing, hesitating, pausing?
- **Body language:** Are their arms crossed, shoulders tense, eyes downcast?
- **Unspoken needs:** What's underneath what they're saying?

This kind of listening takes practice. It takes patience. And yes, it takes emotional maturity. But the payoff is powerful.

Because here's what happens when someone feels truly heard:

- Their defenses begin to soften.
- Their nervous system calms.
- They feel seen, not just heard.
- Connection strengthens.
- Misunderstandings shrink.
- Solutions become easier to find—because now you're on the same side of the issue, not fighting from opposite corners.

That's the power of presence.

Techniques for Active Listening

This isn't about perfection; it's about *intention*. Even just *trying* to understand someone fully can shift the tone of a conversation from combative to collaborative.

◈ *Show You're Listening (Even Without Words)*

- Nod gently from time to time.
- Keep natural eye contact (not a stare-down—just enough to stay connected).
- Stay physically open and turned toward them. That means phone down, laptop shut, body language facing them—not the clock, the door, or your notifications.

Your body says more than your mouth. Let it say, "You have my attention."

◈ *Use Simple Verbal Cues*

Encourage them to keep going. Validate their experience.

- "I hear you."
- "Tell me more about that."
- "That must've been really hard."
- "I didn't realize that; thank you for sharing it."

This isn't about agreeing or fixing—it's about **acknowledging.**

◈ Reflect and Paraphrase

Let them know you're tracking by repeating or rephrasing what they said. This gives them the chance to clarify or deepen the conversation.

- "So, what I'm hearing is... you felt hurt when I didn't follow through."
- "It sounds like you're saying you need more support and feel overwhelmed—am I getting that right?"
- "You're feeling shut out when I make decisions without talking to you first?"

You're not guessing. You're *checking in*. That creates trust.

Obstacles to Active Listening (aka Why It's Hard Sometimes)

Even with the best intentions, active listening can get hijacked. That's okay. Awareness helps.

Here's what gets in the way:

Distractions

Life is loud. Kids need things. Notifications pop up. Your brain is juggling ten tabs.

When distraction strikes, do this:

- Pause.
- Silence the noise.

· Bring your focus back.

Biases and Assumptions

You think you've heard it all before. You roll your eyes internally. You finish their sentence in your head. When that happens:

- · **Remind yourself:** *This is a new moment, even if it sounds familiar.*
- · **Ask yourself:** *What if they're saying something new and I miss it because I'm stuck in the past?*

Emotional Triggers

Their words hit an old wound. Suddenly, you're not listening—you're reacting. When your own "stuff" bubbles up, try this:

- · Breathe. Inhale slowly. Exhale even slower.
- · Ground yourself. Place your feet flat, put your hand on your chest or thigh.
- · Gently remind yourself: *This is about them. I can process my feelings after I've listened.*

The Practice: Presence Over Perfection

You don't need to listen perfectly. You just need to *mean it.*
Set your phone down.
Close your laptop.
Turn toward them.
Give them your eyes. Your ears. Your curiosity. Your heart.

Listening this way—*truly* listening—isn't just a communication skill. It's a gift.

And when you give it consistently, you start to shift the entire energy of your relationship. You create a space where truth feels safe, emotions are honored, and people feel known.

And really—isn't that what we're all reaching for?

Practice Active Listening in Daily Life

Like any skill, active listening gets better the more you use it.

Try these simple starters:

- At dinner, ask your partner or friend how their day was and just listen. No advice. No commentary. Just your attention.
- When your child tells you a story, look them in the eyes and echo back what they said.
- Even in conflict, pause and paraphrase before reacting: "So, you're saying you felt hurt when I forgot to call?"

It's about practicing presence.

Active listening isn't a communication hack—it's a healing practice. It's one of the most powerful gifts you can offer someone: to feel seen, heard, and safe in your presence.

As you get better at listening to others, you'll get better at listening to yourself, too.

Master the Art of Empathetic Communication

Melanie used to think she was being honest, direct, and clear. But the truth was, she often left people feeling dismissed.

When her sister called to vent about a breakup, Melanie would jump in with: "Well, he was kind of a jerk anyway. You're better off."

When her husband opened up about work stress, she'd offer solutions before he finished his sentence: "Just tell your boss you're burned out. It's not that complicated."

She meant well, but something was missing.

Her sister stopped calling. Her husband stopped opening up. And Melanie felt more disconnected than ever.

It wasn't until therapy that she realized the missing ingredient wasn't better advice, it was empathy.

Empathetic communication is what turns a conversation into a connection. It's the moment someone says, "You really get me."

This subchapter will help you bring more heart into your words, especially when it's hard. Whether you're supporting a partner, navigating a tough conversation with a friend, or trying to repair a fractured connection, empathy is what will get you there.

Defining Empathetic Communication

Empathy is all about feeling with someone.

Empathetic communication means

- slowing down to recognize the emotions beneath the words
- validating feelings, not brushing them aside
- shifting the goal from being right or efficient to being real and present

It's no longer just, "Here's what I think." It becomes: "I hear you. I feel how hard this is. I'm with you."

That shift alone can dissolve walls and deepen trust.

Strategies for Empathetic Conversations

Here are some great strategies to get you started with empathy in your conversations:

- **Reflect what you hear and try:**
- "That sounds so frustrating."
- "I can hear how disappointed you are."
- "It makes sense that you'd feel hurt."
- **Stay judgment-free:** Hold back the urge to label, fix, or advise right away. Instead of "You're overreacting," try "That seems like it really got to you."
- **Share carefully:** Sometimes it helps to say, "I've felt

something similar once…" But only if it adds connection, not competition. This isn't the time to one-up or hijack the moment. The focus stays on them.

Practicing Empathy in Difficult Conversations

Empathy is easy when everyone's calm. The test is when emotions rise. Here's how to stay grounded in empathy even when things get tense:

- **Know your triggers:** Melanie learned that when her husband raised a concern, she heard it as criticism. Her instinct? Defend. Yell. Her new approach? Pause. Breathe. Then respond with, "That must've been hard to bring up."
- **Take breaks:** Sometimes, empathy needs space. A simple: "I want to keep talking, but I need five minutes to collect myself," can prevent blowups.
- **Ask open-ended questions:**
- "Can you tell me more about how that made you feel?"
- "What do you need from me right now?"

Nurturing Empathy Over Time

Empathy isn't a one-and-done skill. It's a practice.

Try these daily acts to keep it alive:

- **Reflect:** After a conversation, ask yourself, *Did I respond with empathy or reaction?*

- **Invite feedback:** Ask loved ones, "Do you feel like I under-stand you when we talk?"
- **Keep growing:** Read, journal, or join discussions that stretch your emotional awareness.

Melanie started keeping a "compassion journal." Just one sentence a day: *Who did I connect with today, and how did it feel?*

Over time, those small moments rewired her relationships and her self-awareness.

When you're ready, give it a try. The results speak for themselves:

- It turns communication into care.
- It transforms defensiveness into understanding.
- It lays the foundation for healing even when relationships are bruised.

Because when someone feels safe to be seen, they show you who they really are.

Let's learn to meet them there.

Engage in Constructive Feedback Dialogues

Melanie used to flinch when her husband said, "Can we talk?"

To her, it felt like code for "You've done something wrong." Her stomach would knot, her defenses would rise, and before the conversation even began, she was already preparing her counter-argument.

For years, feedback in their marriage came packaged in frustration, and it usually ended in an argument.

But everything changed when they both learned this truth: Feedback doesn't have to hurt. In fact, when it's done with care and received with openness, it can heal.

The Importance of Feedback in Relationships

Think of feedback like a mirror. It helps you see things you might not notice on your own.

In healthy relationships, feedback shouldn't focus on tearing each other down. Instead, allow it to

- support growth, not demand perfection.
- clarify intentions so the other person doesn't feel attacked.
- create an environment where trust deepens every time you're honest.

When feedback is mutual, respectful, and kind, it builds emotional safety.

Framework for Giving Constructive Feedback

Here's how to deliver feedback in a way that strengthens instead of shatters:

- **Use the "sandwich approach":**
- **Start with a positive:** "I really appreciate how much you've been helping around the house."
- **Offer the feedback:** "I've been feeling a little unheard when I talk about my work stress—can we find time where we both feel present?"
- **End with reassurance:** "I know we're both working on this, and I'm grateful we're having this conversation."
- **Be specific:** Avoid vague complaints like, "You never listen to me." Instead, try: "When I shared how overwhelmed I was yesterday and you were on your phone, I felt dismissed."
- **Choose your timing wisely:** Don't drop feedback bombs mid-argument or right before bed. Instead, say: "Can we chat tomorrow after dinner? There's something on my mind I'd love to share."

Receiving Feedback Gracefully

No one loves being told they've done something wrong, but how you respond matters.

Try these tips:

- Listen without interrupting. Even if it stings, let the person speak.
- Breathe through defensiveness. You don't have to agree immediately. Just understand first.
- Ask questions for clarity: "Can you give me an example of what you mean?" "How did that make you feel?"

Melanie started saying, "Thank you for telling me." Not because it was easy, but because it helped her grow. That simple sentence shifted the energy from conflict to collaboration.

Creating a Feedback Culture

Healthy relationships aren't feedback-free; they're feedback-friendly.

Here's how to create that vibe:

- **Schedule check-ins:** Once a week, ask each other:
- "Is there anything I can do better?"
- "How have we been doing lately?"
- **Keep it mutual:** Remember to use this feedback to grow together.
- **Celebrate progress:** "Hey, I noticed you really paused and listened yesterday when I was upset. That meant a lot." Recognition builds motivation and positivity.

Feedback isn't always fun, but it's always productive. Handled with empathy, it becomes one of the most loving tools in your relationship toolbox.

Use "I" Statements to Express Feelings: Speak Your Truth Without Starting a War

Melanie didn't mean to sound like she was attacking.

But when she said things like, "You never listen to me," or "You're always ignoring what I say," her husband's shoulders would tense up. He'd go quiet, get defensive, or worse, walk away.

Every time she tried to speak up about her feelings, it felt like the conversation exploded before it even began.

It wasn't until therapy that she discovered the magic of "I" statements—a simple shift in words that completely changed the tone and trajectory of her conversations.

Understanding 'I' Statements

"I" statements are deceptively powerful. Why? Because they help you express your emotions without blaming or attacking.

Here's the difference:

- "You don't care about me." (blaming, accusatory)
- "I feel hurt when I don't get a text back after I've reached out a few times." (emotion-focused, specific, non-threatening)

81

See it?

Instead of cornering someone into defense mode, "I" statements open a door for honest dialogue. They

- reduce defensiveness.
- create emotional safety.
- foster personal accountability.
- encourage connection, not conflict.

Crafting Effective "I" Statements

An "I" statement has three key ingredients:

Start with emotion:

- "I feel sad..."
- "I feel frustrated..."
- "I feel disconnected..."

Describe the behavior (not the person):

- "...when you check your phone while I'm talking."
- "...when plans change last-minute and I don't know what's going on."

End with a request or need:

- "Can we agree to have 10 minutes of no-phone time each night?"

· "It would help if we could communicate changes earlier."

Bonus tip: Keep your tone curious, not confrontational.

Practicing "I" Statements in Real Scenarios

Communication rewiring takes practice, especially if you've grown up in an environment like Melanie's, where yelling was the norm.

Try this:

- **Reframe old arguments:** Take a past conflict and rewrite your part using "I" statements.
- Instead of: "You're selfish for not helping with dinner."
- Try: "I feel overwhelmed when I have to manage dinner alone. I'd really appreciate help."
- **Role-play with a partner or friend:** Practicing outside of tense moments builds fluency and comfort.
- **Start small:** Use "I" statements in everyday moments:
- "I feel appreciated when you make coffee in the morning."
- "I feel stressed when the laundry piles up. Can we split it this weekend?"

These little moments reinforce the habit and the trust.

Overcoming Challenges With "I" Statements

Yes, "I" statements feel vulnerable at first. They ask you to own your emotions, to stop blaming, and to step into honesty.

But vulnerability is a superpower in relationships. It creates emotional intimacy, the very thing we're all craving.

Here are a few things to remember:

- You won't get it perfect right away. That's okay. Keep practicing.
- Not everyone will respond perfectly. Be ready to guide the conversation gently back to understanding.
- Use "I" statements even when the other person doesn't. You set the tone.

Melanie once told her therapist, "I feel like the only one changing." Her therapist smiled and said, "One person changing the conversation changes the relationship."

Words can build walls. Or they can build bridges. "I" statements are the first bricks of that bridge—one heartfelt sentence at a time.

Final Thoughts: Speak With Intention, Connect With Heart

Melanie's story reminds us that communication is more than what we say—it's how we say it, why we say it, and who we become in the process.

When Melanie shifted from reactive replies to true active listening, everything changed. Her conversations with her husband softened. The walls they had built started to come down. For the first time in a long time, they felt like they were on the same team again—heard, valued, and connected.

You've now learned the same tools that helped Melanie turn things around, including:

- how to listen actively
- how to communicate with empathy
- how to offer and receive feedback
- how to speak from your own experience using "I" statements

They might seem simple, but when practiced with real intention, they're powerful enough to heal what feels broken, to transform conversations that once felt impossible, and to create the kind of emotional safety every healthy relationship needs.

If Melanie can do it, so can you. One conversation at a time, one moment of real listening at a time—you have the power to build deeper, stronger, more fulfilling connections.

5

Healing From Past Traumas

Charles never thought of himself as someone with trauma.

He wasn't abused. He wasn't abandoned. He went to church every Sunday, got good grades, and did what was expected of him. But emotions? Those were never part of the picture.

In Charles's home growing up, communication wasn't encouraged; it was shut down. If you were having a bad day, you heard, "Tough it out." If you felt overwhelmed, you were told, "Man up." Emotional expression was brushed aside or buried, leaving Charles with no clue how to recognize what he felt, let alone share it.

The trauma Charles experienced wasn't loud. It was silent. Emotional neglect. Emotional avoidance. And that invisible wound followed him into adulthood—sabotaging his relationships without him even realizing it.

In his first marriage, finances and stress turned into battlegrounds. Instead of talking, Charles would disappear into bed for days. Instead of collaborating, he'd explode when pressured. Instead of building intimacy, he built walls.

The problem wasn't that Charles was a bad person. The problem was that Charles had never been taught how to deal with emotions. His trauma had taught him to hide, to fight, or to shut down, but never to feel, never to connect.

This chapter is for the Charles in all of us.

We're going to explore how unseen traumas—the ones that don't always look like trauma—create invisible patterns that sabotage our relationships:

- the shutting down
- the blowing up
- the disappearing when things get hard
- the desperate people-pleasing to avoid confrontation

You don't have to be perfect to be worthy of healing. You just have to be willing.

Let's start there.

Acknowledge Past Traumas Openly: You Can't Heal What You Pretend Doesn't Hurt

Healing begins with honesty, and that honesty starts by acknowledging the emotional wounds we carry—even the ones we were taught to minimize or ignore.

For most of his life, Charles never thought of himself as someone with trauma. Remember, there was no obvious abuse. No dramatic abandonment. He grew up in a well-meaning home that valued faith, success, and strength but discouraged emotional expression.

It wasn't until adulthood, after his marriage began unraveling, that Charles realized something crucial: The emotional neglect he experienced growing up was a form of trauma. It had shaped how he dealt with conflict, vulnerability, and love.

Understanding Trauma

Trauma doesn't always look like violence or abandonment. Sometimes, it looks like this:

- growing up in an emotionally unavailable home
- being told to hide sadness, anger, or fear
- living under expectations of perfection, without room for real feelings
- being loved only when you performed or behaved a certain way

When emotional needs are ignored or dismissed, we learn dangerous lessons about connection and worth. In Charles's case, the trauma manifested in toxic behaviors: shutting down during conflict, stonewalling tough conversations, lashing out defensively, and retreating instead of reaching out.

By understanding his emotional history, Charles could finally stop blaming himself for failing at relationships and start seeing the deeper cause behind his reactions.

The Power of Acceptance

After understanding comes acceptance, and this step is just as critical. Acceptance doesn't mean excusing hurtful experiences. It means acknowledging that they happened, and that your feelings about them are real and valid.

For Charles, acceptance meant releasing the guilt he carried for not knowing how to "be better" at love. He realized he wasn't weak or broken; he was hurt. He was reacting exactly as he had been taught to react.

Acceptance allowed Charles to face his emotions without shame. It gave him permission to be human, to struggle, and to heal.

When you accept your past with compassion, you create the emotional space needed to begin reprocessing old memories, not from a place of judgment, but from a place of understanding.

Creating a Safe Space

Healing isn't something that happens in isolation. It requires safety—a place where you can speak your truth without fear of judgment or punishment.

For Charles, couples therapy provided that first safe space. Inside that small, neutral room, he finally found permission to feel—to stumble through his words, cry without condemnation, and explore the emotions he had buried for decades.

Creating a safe emotional environment, whether in therapy, a trusted friendship, or even a private journal, is essential. Safety encourages honesty. It allows exploration instead of repression and empowers you to touch the deeper wounds you've spent years protecting.

Breaking the Silence

Charles's greatest shift came when he stopped keeping everything inside. Speaking about his childhood, his fears, and his emotional struggles wasn't easy. It felt vulnerable. Exposed. Even terrifying at first.

But every conversation, every attempt to name his experience out loud, chipped away at the loneliness that trauma had built around him.

Breaking the silence did not erase Charles's pain, but it changed it. It connected him to support, understanding, and a growing belief that he didn't have to heal alone.

When you talk about trauma with trusted individuals, it

- eases feelings of isolation.
- validates your experiences.
- builds a network of support that reinforces your healing journey.

You cannot change toxic behaviors if you don't first understand and honor where they come from. Acknowledging your past— openly, compassionately, and safely—is the first and most courageous step toward real, lasting change.

Finding the Right Help—Because Healing Shouldn't Be One-Size-Fits-All

When Charles began therapy, it wasn't love at first session. He sat stiffly on the couch, wondering if he'd say the "wrong" thing. His therapist asked about his childhood, and Charles felt like saying, "Why does that even matter?" But a few weeks in, something was different. For the first time, he wasn't being told how to fix himself; he was learning how to understand himself.

Finding the right kind of support is powerful. It turns healing from a mystery into a process. Let's explore what that process might look like for you.

Types of Therapy: Find Your Fit

Not all therapy is created equal, and that's a good thing. You get to tailor the experience to what you need.

Here are some popular modalities that help with recognizing harmful patterns, building self-awareness, and creating meaningful, lasting connections (Smith Haghighi, 2024):

- **Cognitive behavioral therapy (CBT):** Ideal for identifying and challenging toxic thoughts and behaviors. Great for people who want tools, strategies, and a more structured approach to rewire thought loops.
- **Psychodynamic therapy:** Focuses on exploring childhood, unconscious patterns, and emotional roots. This is powerful if you're noticing repeated issues in your relationships and want to get to the *why* beneath the behavior.
- **Internal family systems (IFS):** Helps you explore the different "parts" of yourself—like the wounded child, the protector, or the critic. This is especially useful if you feel emotionally torn or don't understand why you react the way you do.
- **Emotionally focused therapy (EFT):** Excellent for couples and individuals who struggle with emotional regulation or connection. It dives deep into attachment wounds and helps you learn how to safely bond again.
- **Somatic therapy:** Trauma doesn't just live in the mind; it lives in the body. Somatic work helps you release stored tension, panic, and emotional blocks through body-based techniques like breathwork and movement.

- **Narrative therapy:** You are not your past. This approach helps you reframe the stories you tell about yourself so you can move forward with power and clarity.

Understanding your options can take away some of the fear around starting therapy. You're not "doing it wrong" if one style doesn't click. You're simply discovering what works for *you*.

Finding a Therapist: It's a Relationship, Not a Transaction

Finding the right therapist is like dating, except you get to talk about yourself a lot, and ghosting is totally avoidable if you ask the right questions.

Here's what helps:

- **Look for credentials and specialties:** Trauma-informed. Attachment-based. Licensed. Certified. These words matter when it comes to safety and skill.
- **Consider your comfort:** Do you feel safe sharing with this person? Do you feel judged or supported? Chemistry and safety go hand in hand.
- **Ask questions early:** It's okay to say, "What's your approach to trauma?" or "Have you worked with clients with toxic relationship patterns before?" You're interviewing *them* as much as they're guiding *you*.
- **Trust your instincts:** If something feels off after a few sessions, it's okay to try someone else. The right fit makes all the difference.

You're not being picky, you're choosing who walks with you on your healing journey. That matters.

Group Therapy: Healing Out Loud

Charles never imagined sitting in a circle with strangers would change his life. But group therapy gave him something individual therapy couldn't: proof he wasn't alone.

Group therapy offers:

- **Community:** You realize others have felt what you've felt. That's powerful.
- **Perspective:** You hear others' stories and recognize your own in their words.
- **Courage:** Speaking in a group builds confidence to express your truth.
- **Support:** You celebrate wins together and hold space for the messy middle.

Whether it's a trauma recovery group, a men's group, or a connection circle, there's a unique power in witnessing and being witnessed. Sometimes, another person's vulnerability cracks open your own. And that's where the real healing begins.

Therapy is about being found. Found by your own voice. Found by people who understand. Found by the parts of you that were buried and are finally ready to come up for air.

You deserve support that fits, holds, and honors you. Healing doesn't have to be lonely.

Journaling: Write It Out—Because Your Heart Has Something to Say

When healing from past traumas, emotions can feel overwhelming, tangled, and confusing. Journaling offers a way to untangle those emotions—to give them shape, space, and a voice—without fear of judgment.

For Charles, it was a turning point.

After realizing that emotional neglect had shaped so many of his toxic patterns, Charles still felt stuck. He knew he needed to *feel* his emotions, but years of shutting down had made it almost impossible to even recognize what he was feeling.

His therapist suggested something simple: Start writing. No rules. No structure. Just sit down every night and put a few words on paper.

At first, Charles thought: *What good could scribbling in a notebook do?*

But little by little, something shifted.

Expressive Writing

Journaling became Charles's first safe space with himself.

Unlike conversations, where he often froze up or felt judged, the page had no expectations. He could write anything—his fears, his anger, his sadness—without worrying about how it sounded.

Some nights, it was just a few words: "I feel lost. I don't know what I'm doing."

Other nights, a flood poured out: "I'm terrified that I'm going to screw everything up again. I feel so stupid when I can't talk about money without shutting down."

By writing freely, Charles gave emotions he had spent decades suppressing a way to exist. And once they existed on the page, they became less scary. They became real, manageable, and, eventually, understandable.

Expressive writing helps because

- it allows emotions to flow without interruption or judgment.
- it clarifies feelings that may seem chaotic inside the mind.
- it uncovers hidden patterns and insights, connecting past wounds to present behaviors.

Through his writing, Charles began seeing clear links between the helplessness he felt as a boy and the helplessness that triggered his adult shutdowns.

Tracking Progress

Journaling isn't just about getting emotions out; it's also about seeing how far you've come.

At first, Charles didn't think he was making any progress. Healing felt slow, like swimming upstream wearing a sweater. But one night, flipping back through his notebook, he noticed something different.

Earlier entries were full of panic and confusion. Later entries showed more curiosity and self-compassion: "I froze up again today, but I caught it faster this time. I didn't yell. I asked for a few minutes to calm down. That's new."

Tracking progress through journaling can

- highlight emotional growth that's hard to notice day-to-day.
- remind you that healing isn't linear, but it *is* happening.
- showcase resilience through setbacks and victories.

When he recorded even small wins, Charles could see that every effort—every uncomfortable conversation, every attempt to stay present—mattered.

Prompted Reflection

When emotions feel too big or vague, guided journaling prompts can help focus your writing and make the exploration feel less overwhelming.

Charles's therapist offered simple but powerful prompts to help him dig deeper, such as:

- "When was the first time I remember feeling invisible?"
- "What situations today trigger old feelings of being unsafe?"
- "What would I tell my younger self who felt alone with his feelings?"

These questions didn't just stir up old pain; they provided structure for exploring it safely.

Using prompts can

- target specific traumas or emotional patterns for healing.
- deepen understanding of triggers and reactions.
- offer a safe, guided pathway through difficult memories.

Over time, prompted reflection helped Charles connect the dots between his past and his present, giving him greater emotional awareness and control.

Creating Rituals

Consistency is key in emotional healing. That's why turning journaling into a daily ritual rather than a random, occasional event can be so powerful.

Charles created a simple ritual: Each night before bed, he made a cup of tea, sat in his favorite chair, and wrote for ten minutes. No screens, no distractions, just him, his notebook, and his feelings.

This ritual did more than make journaling a habit; it made it a sacred space. A space where Charles could meet himself with honesty, kindness, and hope.

Creating a journaling ritual can

- build emotional mindfulness into your daily routine.
- deepen your connection to yourself over time.
- foster consistency that strengthens healing and emotional clarity.

Choosing a comfortable spot, setting a calming atmosphere (like lighting a candle or playing soft music), and setting a time each day can help ground this ritual and make it something you look forward to.

Develop a Support Network for Recovery

Healing from emotional trauma doesn't happen in isolation. No matter how strong or independent we think we are, we need connection. We need safe people who can help us carry what feels too heavy alone.

Charles learned this the hard way.

For most of his life, Charles believed that needing support was weakness. In his family, strength meant self-sufficiency, handling your emotions in silence, toughing it out alone.

But during therapy, Charles realized healing was about understanding himself while letting others in.

Identifying Supportive Individuals

The first step for Charles was figuring out who could actually offer real, meaningful support.

Not everyone in his life was equipped to help him heal. Some friends would just tell him to "suck it up" or "focus on the positives." Others would get uncomfortable and change the subject when emotions came up.

But a few, a close friend from college, his therapist, and eventually a trusted coworker, made space for his feelings without trying to fix or dismiss them.

Charles learned to notice the difference:

- Supportive people listened without judgment.
- They validated his feelings, even if they didn't have solutions.
- They treated his emotions as normal, not burdensome.

Choosing to invest in relationships with these individuals gave Charles a safe, nurturing environment where healing could actually take root.

He started to feel seen, accepted, and less alone.

Building Community

Beyond individual relationships, Charles also discovered the power of community.

On his therapist's recommendation, he joined a local men's support group so he had a space specifically for men struggling with emotional expression and relationship challenges.

He was initially uncomfortable, but over time, hearing other men share their fears, mistakes, and pain cracked something open in him.

He wasn't the only one.

In that community, Charles found this:

- understanding that felt deeper than any casual conversation
- shared experiences that mirrored his own struggles
- encouragement that wasn't based on fixing him, but walking alongside him

Being part of a healing community strengthened his recovery. It reminded him that while trauma isolates, healing reconnects.

Communicating Needs

Another vital lesson Charles learned was how to ask for what he needed. Early on, he would expect others to "just know" when he was struggling, and when they didn't, he'd retreat even further.

In therapy, he practiced saying simple but powerful things like this:

- "I'm feeling overwhelmed. Can we just sit together without trying to fix it?"
- "I need someone to listen right now, not solve anything."
- "Can you check in on me later today? It would help me feel supported."

By clearly communicating his emotional needs, Charles gave the people who loved him a real chance to show up in the ways that mattered most.

And every time he asked—every time someone responded with

care—it built trust. It built hope.

Reciprocal Support

Healing also taught Charles that support couldn't just be one-sided.

As he grew stronger, he began offering support to others in his network, too—friends who were going through divorces, coworkers facing anxiety, men in his group opening up for the first time.

By being there for others, Charles deepened his own healing:

- He reinforced empathy, both for himself and for others.
- He stayed connected, even during setbacks.
- He created a culture of mutual care, not silent suffering.

Reciprocal support reminded Charles that healing isn't a race or a competition; it's a relationship. One where giving and receiving create a shared space for growth, compassion, and resilience.

Final Thoughts: You're Healing and That's Brave Work

You've walked a brave path through this chapter, and you've seen it reflected in Charles's story, too.

Charles didn't just recognize his toxic patterns—shutting

down, lashing out, retreating—he faced them head-on. He acknowledged the traumas he didn't even realize he carried. He used tools like therapy, journaling, and building a support network to untangle years of emotional confusion. And little by little, he found healthier ways to feel, to communicate, and to heal.

Just like Charles, you are doing the work.

You've opened doors to your past that were sealed tight. You've started speaking your truth. Maybe you've picked up a pen and journaled through the noise, daring to be honest with yourself. You've looked at your pain with curiosity, not judgment.

That's progress and healing in motion.

And now? It's time to go deeper. Because healing from trauma is also about who you are becoming, it's about choosing, day after day, to respond to life with clarity, compassion, and conscious strength.

The next chapter will guide you into building emotional intelligence—learning to recognize, understand, and manage your emotions with confidence.

You have already proven you have the courage to start. Now it's time to become the person who can love, connect, and lead with emotional strength and self-awareness.

Let's keep going.

6

Building Emotional Intelligence—How to Stop the Damage Before It Starts

Erin never thought of herself as toxic. Intense? Sure. Emotional? Absolutely. But toxic? That word was for other people. The manipulators. The cheaters. The ones who lied and didn't care.

Not her. She cared deeply. That's why she shouted. That's why she slammed cabinet doors and tossed things across the room. That's why, after 10 years of marriage, she found herself yelling things like, "Then go! Just leave! Why are you even here?"

To her, it all made sense.

"He never listens," she told herself. "He always talks over me. I have to scream to be heard."

And every time he walked away during an argument, it only added fuel to the fire. "Fine," she'd snap. "Walk out again. Maybe this time, don't come back."

So, when her husband finally didn't come back—when he calmly, quietly, filed for divorce—Erin was blindsided. She didn't know how to process it. All she knew was that the house suddenly felt very, very quiet. And that silence became a mirror she hadn't wanted to look into.

This chapter is for anyone who, like Erin, is ready to really look. Because here's the truth: Many of us don't realize we're showing up in harmful ways until it's too late. And that's not because we're bad people, it's because we've never learned emotional intelligence.

Emotional intelligence (EQ) is the ability to recognize your emotions, manage them skillfully, and respond to others with empathy and awareness. It's what keeps our reactions from becoming explosions. It's what helps us stay present during conflict instead of shutting down, lashing out, or spiraling. And it's absolutely essential for building healthy, lasting relationships.

In this chapter, we're going to take a deep, honest look at how to build your emotional intelligence step by step. We'll walk with Erin as she begins to do the same.

EQ won't change your past, but it can transform your future. And as Erin will begin to discover, it can help you stop the damage before it starts.

Ready to start this journey?

Identify and Label Emotions Accurately

Before Erin could even begin to change how she reacted in her relationship, she had to learn something surprisingly basic but life-changing: how to name what she was feeling.

For years, she used catch-all words like angry, frustrated, or fine to describe her emotional state. But beneath every scream-ing rage or slammed door was something more specific— something she couldn't name at the time. Was she feeling unheard? Hurt? Afraid of abandonment? Trapped? Without clarity, her emotions spilled out chaotically, leaving her hus-band exhausted and disconnected.

This is why learning to identify and accurately label emotions is a foundational step in building emotional intelligence. It gives us a map—a way to navigate the storm before it wrecks the house. Let's explore how this works in practice.

Understanding Emotion Types

We often think in broad strokes: sad, mad, happy. But emotions are layered and nuanced. For instance, anger can be a cover for shame, fear, insecurity, or grief. Erin's outbursts weren't just "anger." They were often the result of feeling dismissed, invisible, or powerless.

When you understand the types of emotions—primary ones like fear, joy, sadness, anger, surprise, and disgust—you gain a lens for deeper self-awareness. And with that lens, you can better understand why you're reacting the way you are.

In Erin's case, labeling her anger as "abandoned" or "not enough" helped her approach her pain with curiosity instead of combustion.

Using Emotion Journals

One of the most effective ways to begin labeling emotions is through journaling. Writing down what you feel, when you feel it, and what triggered it, can expose the emotional loops you've been stuck in.

Erin started keeping a simple emotion journal after her separation. Every day, she jotted down the following:

- what happened
- what she felt
- what she needed but didn't express

Over time, she noticed patterns. Her rage often followed moments of vulnerability, like when she tried to share a need and it was dismissed. This helped her realize: her explosions were defensive reactions to unspoken hurt.

Emotion journals allow you to slow the emotional process down, examine it, and learn from it rather than just relive it.

Practicing Emotion Check-Ins

Before Erin rebuilt her relationships, she had to rebuild her awareness. She set alarms on her phone to pause three times a day and ask herself these questions:

- *What am I feeling right now?*
- *Why might I be feeling it?*
- *What do I need?*

These emotion check-ins helped her track emotional shifts before they turned into blowups. They also helped her spot the difference between external triggers and internal narratives. By simply noticing, she began to make space between feeling and reacting. That space became her power.

Developing Emotional Vocabulary

Emotional maturity thrives on language. The more words you have to describe your inner world, the more easily you can connect with others. Instead of saying, "I'm just mad," Erin learned to say, "I'm feeling rejected and overwhelmed because I'm afraid I don't matter right now."

That shift changed everything. When we can name it, we can tame it. And when we communicate clearly, we invite understanding instead of defensiveness.

Start by expanding your emotional vocabulary. Explore lists of feelings and keep them handy. You can even print or download a "feelings wheel" on your device to help. Practice replacing vague statements with specific ones. Over time, your inner world will feel less like a storm and more like a conversation.

The Bottom Line

Labeling your emotions accurately isn't about overanalyzing; it's about honoring your truth and communicating with clarity. Erin didn't learn this overnight, but each time she named a feeling with honesty, she loosened the grip of the chaos that once controlled her.

And that's where real change begins.

Practice Self-Regulation Strategies

By the time Erin began her emotional healing journey, she had one painful truth to reckon with: She had never learned how to calm herself down. Her go-to response when emotions surged? Yell. Slam something. Threaten to leave or push him to.

It wasn't that she wanted to explode. She simply didn't know what else to do with the tidal wave inside her.

That's where self-regulation comes in.

Self-regulation is the ability to manage your emotional reactions so they don't hijack your relationships or your peace. Let's walk through the key self-regulation strategies that helped Erin go from constant chaos to emotional control.

Coping Mechanisms: Learning to Soothe Yourself

The first time Erin felt her blood pressure spike during a tough conversation after her separation, her instinct was to lash out. But instead of yelling, she excused herself, walked into the bathroom, splashed cold water on her face, and breathed. That simple pause? It changed everything.

Coping mechanisms are the tools you use to soothe your nervous system in moments of emotional overwhelm. These can include:

- deep breathing exercises
- grounding techniques (like feeling your feet on the floor or naming five things you see)
- progressive muscle relaxation
- listening to calming music
- taking a short walk

When Erin began to use these tools regularly, she noticed something remarkable: Her emotional storms didn't last as long. And she no longer felt powerless inside them.

Learning to self-soothe doesn't require you to suppress emotions. Instead, it focuses on holding them without letting them explode.

Mindfulness Techniques for Regulation

Mindfulness was a turning point for Erin. At first, she found it frustrating to sit still. But once she realized that mindfulness wasn't about "emptying her mind" but noticing her thoughts without judgment, everything shifted.

When she practiced being present in her body—even for five minutes a day—it helped her stay grounded during emotionally intense moments.

Here are a few simple mindfulness practices you can try:

- **Box breathing:** Inhale for 4, hold for 4, exhale for 4, hold for 4.
- **Body scans:** Quietly observe tension or emotion in each part of your body.
- **Mindful pausing:** Before responding, take 3 deep breaths and check in with yourself:
- *What am I really feeling?*
- *What do I want to say—kindly?*

Mindfulness helps create space between feeling and action. And in that space, Erin began choosing responses over reactions—a power that slowly changed the way she related to others.

Setting Emotional Boundaries

Erin used to think honest communication was letting it all out, no matter how messy. But she came to understand that honesty without boundaries can become emotional dumping.

Setting emotional boundaries doesn't mean you shut down or bottle things up. It means you express emotions in ways that don't cause harm—to you or others. Here are a few examples:

- "I need a minute to cool down before I talk."
- "I'm feeling overwhelmed, and I want to revisit this when I'm calmer."
- "I care about resolving this, but not by yelling."

By creating space and using these boundaries, Erin learned how to protect her emotional energy and keep her conversations productive.

Boundaries aren't walls. They're doors with hinges, and they are designed to open when it's safe.

Dealing With Triggers

There were moments when Erin felt hijacked by emotion without fully knowing why—until she learned to identify her triggers. One of her biggest? Feeling dismissed. It reminded her of being silenced in childhood, which is why her husband talking over her hit so deep.

Recognizing a trigger is like turning on a light in a dark room. It gives you the power to

- pause and ground before reacting.
- speak to the real emotion underneath the surface.
- choose strategies that support resolution instead of escalation.

Erin began keeping a "trigger tracker" in her journal. She began writing down what situations triggered her, what emotion arose, and how she responded. Over time, this made her reactions predictable and manageable.

When we understand our triggers, we take back our power. We stop letting the past write the script for the present.

The Bottom Line

Self-regulation isn't about being perfect. It's about being conscious. Erin didn't change overnight, but each moment she chose to pause, to breathe, to respond instead of react, she was reclaiming her power and rewriting her relationship story.

And you can, too.

Enhance Social Awareness Skills

For most of her marriage, Erin saw herself as the emotionally expressive one—the one who felt deeply. But what she didn't realize was that while she was busy reacting to her own emotions, she rarely noticed what her husband was feeling.

His slumped shoulders, quiet sighs, or long silences after their arguments weren't signs of indifference. They were signs of defeat. Signs Erin missed because she wasn't paying attention.

Social awareness is the ability to read the emotional climate of your relationship. It means understanding not just your feelings, but also the feelings of those around you. When you enhance this skill, you gain access to emotional data that words don't always reveal.

Let's take a closer look at how Erin learned to become more socially attuned and how you can too.

Active Observation Techniques

Erin's therapist once gave her a simple assignment: Next time you're with someone, say nothing for 30 seconds and just observe.

At first, it felt weird. But soon, she noticed how much people say without speaking—how crossed arms, furrowed brows, or shifting feet can tell an entire story. Her husband used to press his lips together when he was trying not to cry. She had missed that—again and again.

Active observation means tuning in to the following:

- facial expressions
- tone of voice
- posture
- gestures
- eye contact (or lack thereof)

The more Erin practiced noticing, the more empathetic she became. She stopped assuming. She started asking. And she learned that paying attention is one of the purest forms of love.

Empathy Development Exercises

Empathy is a feeling and a skill you can build. Erin began practicing empathy by doing exercises like these:

- **"Walk in Their Shoes" journaling:** writing from her husband's point of view after a conflict
- **Emotional mirroring:** Noticing someone's emotion and trying to reflect it gently ("You seem really overwhelmed, do you want to talk about it?")
- **Daily empathy check-ins:** asking someone close, "How are you really feeling today?" and listening

These exercises rewired Erin's emotional lens. Instead of assuming her husband's silence meant he didn't care, she began to wonder if it meant he didn't feel safe.

That shift—from assumption to curiosity—is the essence of empathy.

Social Context Understanding

There were moments when Erin would launch into a melt-down... in public, at dinner, in front of friends. Looking back, she realized that her emotions often overshadowed the moment, making others uncomfortable or defensive.

Social context awareness is the ability to assess when and how to express emotions. It means asking yourself:

- *Is this the right time and place for this conversation?*
- *What's the emotional state of the other person right now?*
- *Am I responding to this moment, or dragging in unresolved pain from another?*

Understanding context helps you handle emotional moments with grace and timing. Erin began pausing before engaging in tough conversations, checking both her own state and the environment. That pause gave her the chance to recalibrate and preserve connection.

Listening Without Judgment

Erin had a habit of interrupting. Not out of rudeness, but because she felt so urgently misunderstood. But the result was that her husband often shut down, feeling like there was no room for his truth.

When Erin began practicing non-judgmental listening, everything changed. She learned to

- stay quiet until the other person finished their thought.
- reflect back what she heard without adding commentary.
- breathe through the discomfort of hearing something that triggered her.

She didn't always agree with what her husband said, but she stopped trying to win. And in doing so, she started building something far more valuable: trust.

Listening without judgment is a gift. It tells the other person, "You are safe to be fully yourself here."

The Bottom Line

Social awareness is about presence. When Erin stopped reacting and started noticing, asking, and empathizing, her world expanded. She began to see not just her pain, but the pain she had missed in others.

And in that awareness, healing began.

Utilize Relationship Management Techniques

When Erin began the hard work of healing, she wanted to avoid future blowups, but she also wanted to become someone who could build healthy relationships, not just survive them.

For the first time, she asked herself: *What does it mean to actually manage a relationship well—not just react to it?*

Relationship management is the capstone skill of emotional intelligence. It's what turns awareness into action, and connection into a conscious practice. Let's explore how Erin applied key relationship management techniques and how you can do the same.

Conflict Resolution Frameworks

In her past, Erin handled conflict like a tornado—emotions flying, nothing spared, and nothing resolved. But when she learned about structured conflict resolution frameworks (like pause–reflect–express–request), she realized conflict didn't have to be war; it could be a bridge.

A simple framework Erin adopted looked like this:

- **Pause:** Step back to cool down before reacting.
- **Reflect:** Ask yourself, *What am I feeling? What do I need?*
- **Express:** Use "I" statements to express her needs calmly.
- **Request:** Make a clear, kind ask for what could help repair or move forward.

This structure gave her the clarity she never had during arguments. It helped her replace emotional chaos with intentional communication, and that shift alone helped change her next relationship into a safer space for honesty.

Frameworks don't eliminate conflict; they give it purpose and direction.

Collaborative Communication Strategies

Before, Erin believed that if she didn't "win" an argument, she'd lose herself. But what she learned over time is that collaboration creates more lasting power than control ever could.

Collaborative communication means

- listening to understand, not just to respond.
- focusing on the problem, not the person.
- using language like "How can we work through this to-gether?" instead of "You always...".
- staying open to solutions, even if they aren't yours.

Erin began to frame conflicts as shared challenges instead of personal attacks. This subtle shift turned confrontations into conversations. Her new mindset helped her and her future partner approach tough topics like a team, not rivals.

Feedback Mechanisms

One of the hardest things for Erin was learning how to give and receive feedback without becoming defensive. In the past, any critique felt like rejection. But as her emotional intelligence grew, she saw feedback for what it was: an invitation to grow.

She and her new partner eventually created a rhythm where they would check in every Sunday:

- "What's something I did well this week?"
- "What's something I could do better?"
- "Is there anything you're needing more or less of?"

These mini-feedback loops helped catch small issues before they became resentments. They also built trust because both people knew they were free to speak without fear.

Feedback, done right, is less about judgment and more about strengthening the relationship.

Celebrating Relationship Wins

In her old dynamic, Erin focused on what was missing—what her partner wasn't doing, how she felt neglected. She never paused to notice what was working. Gratitude was absent.

Now, she's intentional about celebrating small wins:

- "Thanks for checking in with me earlier—I felt really cared for."
- "That was a hard conversation, and I'm proud of how we handled it."
- "I love how we make time for each other even when life is busy."

These acknowledgments shift the emotional tone of a relationship. They create warmth, reinforce trust, and remind both people why they're in it together.

Celebration isn't frivolous; it's fuel for connection.

The Bottom Line

Relationship management should always focus on presence and practice. Erin didn't change her patterns by accident. She built new ones—deliberately, patiently, and with compassion.

By using conflict frameworks, collaborative dialogue, feedback loops, and celebration rituals, she began to feel something she hadn't felt in years: empowered and connected.

That's the beauty of emotional intelligence. It doesn't just change your inner world—it transforms your relationships from the inside out.

Final Thoughts: From Chaos to Clarity

Erin didn't think she was the problem. She thought she was passionate. Misunderstood. Just trying to be heard.

But in the silence that followed her husband's departure, she finally saw the patterns she had been too reactive to notice and too afraid to name. The screaming wasn't strength. The threats weren't power. The emotional explosions weren't truth, they were unprocessed pain.

And so, she began again.

She learned to name her emotions instead of hurling them. She practiced self-regulation, calming her nervous system instead of fueling the fire. She paid attention to others' emotions, recognizing the cues she had once ignored. And she developed the tools to manage relationships—not through control but through curiosity, care, and conscious effort.

It wasn't easy. It wasn't instant. But it was everything.

Because now? Erin isn't just surviving her relationships. She's nurturing them. Respecting them. And most importantly, she's respecting herself. And that's where your path is heading, too.

Emotional intelligence is only the beginning. In the next chapter, we'll explore one of the most powerful ways to protect your peace and sustain meaningful connection: setting and maintaining healthy boundaries.

Because love without boundaries isn't intimacy—it's enmeshment. And healing without boundaries doesn't last—it collapses under the weight of old patterns.

Let's keep going. You're doing the work. You're becoming the version of yourself you were always meant to be. And that deserves to be protected.

Let's talk boundaries.

7

Setting and Maintaining Healthy Boundaries

Alana had always prided herself on being strong, capable, and in control.

At 45, she was a successful pediatrician, respected by peers and patients alike. She had been married for two decades, raised three children, and carried the kind of presence that made people sit up a little straighter. Her mother raised her to be empowered: "Never let anyone walk over you," she used to say. And Alana took that to heart. But her mother's version of empowerment had sharp edges. She made everyone's business her business. Boundaries? Those were for people who didn't care enough.

It worked, but only for a while.

Until her adult children came to her one by one. They weren't angry. They were careful. They talked about how they felt they could never fully breathe around her. That they never had privacy growing up. That even now, she seemed to be hovering, questioning, steering every decision. They were scared to share certain things with her—scared of her reaction, of her judgment, of feeling bulldozed.

And when Alana finally opened up to her husband about all of this, he was quiet. Not because he didn't care, but because, deep down, he had been afraid to be honest with her, too.

Alana had always thought boundaries were walls people used to shut others out. But now, she was starting to see that the opposite might be true: that boundaries are actually what make closeness possible. That without them, love gets tangled with control, protection gets mistaken for dominance, and connection suffers under the weight of too much intrusion.

In this chapter, we're going to explore the art of setting and maintaining healthy boundaries. We'll look at how boundaries aren't just lines we draw with others, but also internal markers that let us know when we feel safe, seen, and respected enough to show up with authenticity. For Alana, that meant learning how to create emotional safety for herself before she could soften, trust, or truly let love flow.

We'll also explore how to recognize and honor the boundaries of others, even when it challenges your habits or makes you feel left out. Because healthy relationships aren't built through control—they're built through mutual respect and trust.

Define Personal Boundaries Clearly: Clarity Creates Connection Without Compromise

For most of her life, Alana believed she was protecting and guiding her family. She never thought of herself as controlling or toxic—just involved. Deeply involved. But when her grown children gently told her they didn't feel like they had any personal space or choice, and her husband admitted that he felt the same, Alana was forced to face a truth she hadn't seen before. She had never clearly defined her own boundaries or respected anyone else's.

Understanding Boundaries

Boundaries are more than just rules. They're the invisible lines that separate where *you* end and someone else begins. They define your emotional space, physical comfort, and mental clarity. Alana had spent years making decisions for everyone, assuming that closeness meant constant access. But true closeness can only exist when both people feel safe being themselves—without fear of being pushed, judged, or overruled.

When we lack boundaries, relationships can become enmeshed or distant—either we lose ourselves in others, or we push them away to preserve our sense of self. Boundaries help preserve individual identity *within* connection. They tell others how we want to be treated, and they allow us to interact with empathy without losing emotional balance.

126

Types of Boundaries

As Alana began to reflect, she started to notice how many types of boundaries she had blurred without even realizing it. Let's look at the different types of boundaries:

- **Physical boundaries** include your personal space and comfort with touch. Alana was affectionate with her children, but even as adults, she'd barge into their rooms uninvited or insist on hugging when they didn't feel like it.
- **Emotional boundaries** protect your thoughts, feelings, and inner world. Alana often dismissed her children's opinions if they didn't align with hers, believing she "knew better." But in doing so, she silenced their emotional truths.
- **Digital boundaries** include your right to privacy online or through personal devices. Alana once read her son's private messages on social media "just to make sure he was okay." In her mind, it was loving. But to him, it was a betrayal of trust. On another occasion, she demanded her husband hand over his phone so she could "check his messages" completely disregarding his privacy or trust.

When we don't understand the different kinds of boundaries, we risk stepping into someone else's space without permission, and that breaks down trust fast.

Identifying Your Needs

For Alana, the turning point came when she asked herself: *What do I need in order to feel safe, open, and loved?*

She realized she had been operating from a place of constant control because she didn't feel safe letting go. She feared that loosening her grip meant losing her family. But what she really needed was emotional safety—to be heard, accepted, and respected for who she truly was, not just for what she could control or manage.

Recognizing your needs is the first step to setting boundaries. What makes you feel anxious? What leaves you feeling resentful, drained, or invisible? These emotions are signals that a boundary may be missing. And once you become aware of them, you can start to clearly communicate what feels right and what doesn't.

Clarity in this process empowers you to engage in relationships with authenticity, not anxiety.

The Importance of Flexibility

Boundaries aren't set in stone. They're living, breathing agreements that evolve as we grow and change.

At first, Alana went from being overly involved to pulling away completely, worried she'd mess things up again. But that wasn't the solution either. Instead, she began talking openly with her family. She asked questions. She listened. She started saying things like, "I want to give you space. Please let me know how I can support you without overstepping."

That's the power of flexible boundaries: They adjust with time, while still protecting your emotional well-being.

As relationships mature, boundaries might need to be revisited. A friend might become a partner. A child might become an adult. A quiet partner may finally speak up. Flexibility lets us honor these shifts without losing connection.

And when you define your boundaries clearly, you give others the freedom to show up honestly, too. You're not creating walls. You're opening doors—just with a respectful knock first.

Communicate Boundaries Assertively

When Alana first started to recognize her need for boundaries, the hardest part wasn't identifying them—it was talking about them. As a pediatrician, she was used to giving orders, fixing problems, and staying in control. But opening up about her feelings? That was new terrain.

After years of being seen as "intimidating," Alana had to learn how to express herself in a way that didn't shut people down, but also didn't shrink her truth. That's where assertive communication came in.

The Assertiveness Framework

Assertiveness isn't aggression. It's not about demanding or dominating; it's about being clear, respectful, and grounded in your truth. It's the difference between saying, "You're always disrespectful!" and "I need to feel heard when I'm sharing something important."

When Alana sat down with her daughter after their difficult conversation, she wanted to respond with defensiveness. But instead, she practiced being assertive. She said, "I didn't realize how my actions were affecting you. I want to respect your space. Can you help me understand what that looks like for you?"

That slight shift created a new dynamic—one where honesty didn't equal hostility, and everyone had a voice.

Assertive communication sets the tone for healthier relationships. It lets others know what you need, while also inviting their input. It turns boundaries into conversations, not ultimatums.

Using "I" Statements

One of the most powerful tools in Alana's shift was learning to use "I" statements—a simple technique that changes the whole energy of a conversation:

· Instead of saying, "You never let me help!" She tried, "I

feel left out when I'm not included in decisions."
· Instead of, "You're always in my space!" Her daughter said, "I feel overwhelmed when you come into my room without knocking."

These statements focus on the speaker's experience, not the other person's faults. They invite understanding rather than triggering defensiveness. And most importantly, they make emotional expression safe.

Practicing "I" statements helps you get comfortable with vulnerability. It's not always easy, especially if you grew up in a home where emotions were ignored or weaponized. But the more you practice, the more natural it becomes to say, "This is what I need to feel safe and respected."

Practicing Active Listening

Setting boundaries is a two-way street. You can't just speak— you also have to listen.

Alana realized that part of her old communication style involved jumping in, correcting, and assuming. So, she began slowing down and listening during conversations with her children and husband. She didn't interrupt. She made space, and that changed everything.

When we actively listen, we give someone our full attention. It means saying things like,
   "What I'm hearing is..." or "That sounds really important to

you—can you tell me more?"

It's not about agreeing with everything but valuing the other person's experience. And when both people feel heard, boundary-setting becomes collaborative instead of confrontational.

For Alana, this meant truly understanding why her children needed digital privacy, or why her husband didn't always want to talk things through immediately. Listening helped her meet their needs without abandoning her own.

Setting Consequences

Of course, even the clearest boundary won't mean much without follow-through. That's why it's essential to communicate consequences when lines are crossed—not as a punishment, but as a way to reinforce your emotional safety.

Alana learned to say things like: "If I feel shut down during this conversation, I'll need to take a break and return to it later."

Consequences establish accountability. They say boundaries matter. If it's not respected, there will be a response.

When clearly communicated, consequences don't damage relationships—they protect them. They show that you're serious about your needs and serious about staying in connection with respect.

Learning to communicate boundaries assertively takes time. But every conversation builds courage. Every moment of honesty builds trust. And every clear statement brings you closer to the relationships you deserve—ones built not on fear or control, but on mutual care, clarity, and freedom.

Respect Others' Boundaries Reciprocally

Alana was beginning to see the truth that had once escaped her: Setting her own boundaries was only half the equation. The other half—equally important—was learning to honor the boundaries of others. That part was harder because it meant stepping back. Letting go. And realizing that love doesn't require control—it requires trust.

As her children became adults and started voicing their limits, Alana had to face some uncomfortable moments. Her instinct was to say, "But I'm just trying to help," or "You'll thank me later." But now, she was learning that respect means listening without defensiveness—and sometimes, adjusting your behavior even when it stings.

Recognizing Boundaries

To begin respecting others' boundaries, you have to be aware they exist. For years, Alana had missed the subtle signs: her daughter closing her bedroom door more often, her son taking longer to respond to texts, her husband sighing quietly during conversations. None of it was loud, but all of it mattered.

133

Boundaries aren't always stated directly. Sometimes, they're hinted at through body language, tone, or even silence. Learning to notice these cues is a skill that deepens empathy and shows care.

When you recognize and value someone else's limits, you help create a relationship culture grounded in respect. And when people feel respected, they're more likely to open up and stay connected.

Asking for Clarification

Boundaries aren't one-size-fits-all. What feels okay to one person might feel intrusive to another. That's why, when in doubt, the best move is simple: ask.

After her son gently mentioned he felt overwhelmed when she checked in too often, Alana asked, "What would feel better for you in terms of how often I reach out?" That one question changed the tone of their entire relationship. It showed she wasn't just tolerating his boundary—she was trying to understand it.

Asking for clarification doesn't mean you've done something wrong. It means you care enough to get it right. And in doing so, you show the other person that their comfort and voice matter.

Clear communication about boundaries prevents hurt, builds transparency, and reduces resentment. It also fosters mutual trust because both people know they can speak up and be heard.

Being Accountable for Violations

Even with the best intentions, we're all going to misstep. We'll say too much. Ask the wrong question. Push a little too far. What matters most is what we do next.

Alana had a moment like this when her daughter found out she'd casually mentioned a personal situation to a colleague. Alana didn't think it was a big deal until she saw her daughter's face. Instead of brushing it off, Alana took a breath and said, "I'm sorry. I didn't realize that was private for you. I'll be more careful moving forward."

Taking responsibility doesn't make you weak—it makes you trustworthy. It tells the other person: "Your boundaries matter to me, and I'll learn from this."

Being accountable for a boundary violation can open the door to healing and even strengthen the relationship. It allows for honest reflection and deeper understanding on both sides.

Creating a Mutual Boundary Agreement

Healthy relationships aren't built on one-sided rules. They're collaborative. That's why creating mutual boundary agreements can be one of the most powerful tools in any relationship—whether with a partner, child, friend, or colleague.

These agreements are essentially conversations where both people share what they need to feel safe, respected, and loved. For Alana and her husband, this meant establishing new rhythms, such as not discussing difficult topics late at night, respecting privacy, and agreeing on quiet time after work. For her children, it meant creating shared expectations about visits, texts, and space.

When boundaries are co-created, everyone feels seen. It's about partnership.

You're not just saying, "Here's what I need." You're also asking, "What do you need from me?" And that question—that invitation—is the foundation of emotional intimacy.

Learning to respect others' boundaries isn't about walking on eggshells. Instead, it centers around walking with them, side by side, in mutual care and consent.

Reassess Boundaries as Relationships Evolve

Alana thought boundaries were something you set once, like installing a fence. Build it, reinforce it, and you're done. But as her children entered adulthood and her marriage entered a quieter, more reflective chapter, she realized something essential: Boundaries aren't static—they're living things. They breathe, shift, and stretch as our relationships and roles change.

The truth is, what kept a relationship safe and thriving five years ago might not serve the same purpose today. To stay connected and emotionally well, boundaries must be revisited and redefined over time.

Recognizing Change

The first step in reassessing boundaries is noticing when the dynamic of a relationship shifts.

Alana had always been the helper, the planner, the voice of reason. But when her youngest daughter moved into her own apartment and started making big life decisions independently, Alana felt... unneeded. And with that discomfort came a temptation to lean back in—to take control, to ask probing questions, to stay involved.

But something inside her paused. She realized that her role was changing, and so were her daughter's needs. Her previous boundary of "always being available" needed to be replaced with one that allowed for more space and trust.

Change is a natural part of life—children grow up, marriages deepen or go through stress, careers evolve, health shifts. Recognizing those transitions gives us the opportunity to adapt—not to control, but to support.

Open Dialogue About Change

Once you notice change, the next step is to talk about it—with openness, curiosity, and compassion.

Alana had a heart-to-heart with her husband after noticing a growing emotional distance between them. She said, "I think we've both changed a lot over the years. I'd like to talk about what we each need now to feel connected and respected."

That kind of invitation to dialogue doesn't just update the terms of the relationship; it strengthens it. It shows that you're not clinging to old roles or assumptions, but showing up with fresh awareness and a willingness to grow together.

Discussing boundary changes builds trust. It sends a message: "I care enough about us to ask what's working, what's not, and what we might need to do differently."

Monitoring Personal Feelings

Sometimes, the most honest signals that a boundary needs to shift come from inside you.

Alana started noticing subtle feelings—resentment when her daughter ignored her texts, exhaustion from saying yes to too many favors, guilt when she needed alone time. These feelings weren't problems; they were messages.

Checking in with yourself regularly—asking, *Does this still feel okay? Do I feel respected? Do I feel connected?*—is an essential practice in boundary work. Emotional discomfort, irritability, or even withdrawal can be clues that your boundaries need adjusting.

Self-awareness isn't selfish; it's self-preserving. And it's how you begin to communicate your evolving needs clearly and kindly.

Adjusting Together

Boundaries don't have to be adjusted in isolation. In fact, the healthiest boundaries are often redefined in partnership.

Alana and her adult son had a conversation that started with tension—he felt like she wasn't as present anymore. She felt like he didn't need her. But as they talked, they discovered something beautiful: both wanted connection, just in a new way.

They decided to schedule weekly check-ins instead of random texts and to have more in-person time when possible. This was less about rules—they were agreements. Mutually designed and mutually respected.

Adjusting boundaries together protects the relationship while enriching it. It says: "We're evolving, and I want our connection to evolve too."

As Alana learned, boundaries aren't about rigidity. They're about responsiveness. They're not a fixed blueprint—they're a growing map.

When you honor change, communicate openly, reflect honestly, and adjust collaboratively, you give your relationships the space they need to thrive—not just in one season, but across a lifetime.

Final Thoughts: The Courage to Draw the Line—and Cross It With Love

Alana didn't change overnight. She didn't suddenly become an expert in boundary-setting or a perfect communicator. What she did do—courageously, imperfectly—was begin.

She started noticing how her desire to protect had sometimes overshadowed her ability to connect. She listened, not just to her family, but to herself. She began speaking up, not with defensiveness, but with honesty. And most of all, she learned to give space, not as a form of distance, but as an invitation for deeper trust.

Her relationships didn't fall apart. They evolved. Her children started opening up more. Her marriage found new softness. She discovered that boundaries weren't barriers to love—they were the very foundation of it.

Alana's journey is a mirror for many of us. Whether you've struggled to draw a line or been afraid to speak your needs, this chapter reminds you: It's never too late to set a boundary. It's never too late to choose mutual respect over silent resentment. It's never too late to create relationships where everyone feels safe, seen, and supported—including you.

As we move into the next chapter, we'll explore what it means to cultivate empathy and compassion because boundaries and empathy go hand in hand. When you understand yourself, you're better equipped to understand others. And when you lead with compassion, even the hardest conversations can become bridges instead of walls.

Let's walk that bridge together.

8

Cultivating Empathy and Compassion

Roger used to think he had it all figured out.

The quintessential bachelor, he wore his independence like a tailored suit—polished, proud, and impossible to wrinkle. At 25, his charm and carefree spirit were magnetic. At 35, he was still "playing the field." By 40, his friends started settling down, but Roger shrugged—he had time. Now in his 50s, sitting across from his therapist, he's beginning to realize that time isn't waiting. A long string of relationships—some passionate, some peaceful, none permanent—had all unraveled. One common thread? Him.

Commitment issues? Maybe. Control issues? Absolutely. But it never felt like control to Roger. It felt like boundaries. Logical, reasonable, and normal. When a girlfriend asked to leave a toothbrush at his place, he said, "Sure." But when she mentioned needing a drawer? He laughed her off. "Adults have their own spaces," he'd say, masking fear with sarcasm.

His go-to lines were always laced with humor:

- "Come on now, you're an independent woman—no need to shack up with me."
- "Marriage? Good Lord, girl—pump those brakes."

The truth, buried deep beneath the banter, was this: Roger had watched his father lose everything—his business, his pride, his identity, his home—when Roger's mother left and took what she could. In Roger's eyes, vulnerability looked like weakness. Sharing felt like sacrifice. And love? That was a transaction that rarely ended well for the man.

Only recently, through the slow, steady work of therapy, has Roger begun to ask the harder question: *What if I've been so busy protecting myself that I never learned how to love someone fully? Could I be portraying toxic behaviors?*

This chapter is about that very question and the skills that help us answer it differently.

Whether you see pieces of Roger in yourself or in someone you've loved, this chapter will walk you through the foundations of cultivating empathy and compassion. These aren't just "nice-to-haves" in relationships; they are the roots of trust, the balm for conflict, and the bridges we build when we want love to last and toxicity to vanish.

We'll explore the following:

- **Perspective-taking:** the ability to step out of your own

head and see through someone else's eyes
- **Emotional listening:** how to hear not just the words, but the heart behind them
- **Empathetic responses:** how to respond with care, not defensiveness
- **Kindness in action:** what it looks like to turn understanding into behavior

And yes—we'll keep Roger with us as we go. His story is far from over. Like many of us, he's learning that healing isn't about shame—it's about growing into the person you were always capable of becoming.

Let's begin.

Engage in Perspective-Taking Exercises

Roger never thought of himself as selfish. In his mind, he was simply practical—rational, even. He didn't yell. He didn't cheat. He always paid for dinner. In his version of reality, that was enough. But now, in therapy, he's facing a hard truth: He never really saw his partners. Not fully. Not from their perspective.

Empathy isn't only about feeling for someone; it's about seeing from their point of view. When we engage in perspective-taking exercises, we challenge the story we've always told ourselves and make room for a deeper, more connected narrative.

Understanding Different Perspectives

Roger once dated a woman who, after eight months, asked if she could leave a few things at his place—a drawer for her clothes, a hairbrush, some tea she liked. He panicked. "Let's not play house, we aren't children," he joked, dismissing her with a laugh. At the time, he told himself she was moving too fast. Now, in therapy, he replays that moment with fresh eyes.

What might she have been feeling? Vulnerable? Hopeful? Maybe even rejected when he laughed. What message did he send, however unintentionally? "You don't belong here."

Perspective-taking begins with these kinds of questions. When we step into someone else's shoes—even hypothetically—we begin to dismantle the walls between "me" and "you." We stop assuming and start understanding. This shift alone can turn conflict into connection.

Role-Playing Scenarios

Roger's therapist suggested something he'd never done before: role-play. At first, it felt silly. But when she asked him to speak as if he were his ex-girlfriend, explaining how she felt in that toothbrush-and-tea moment, something clicked.

He softened.

He said things like, "I just wanted to feel at home when I'm here with you." And for the first time, he heard what she might've been trying to communicate all along.

145

Role-playing isn't about performance. It's about practice. When you speak from someone else's emotional space—even awkwardly—it invites your heart to stretch. It increases emotional intelligence and prepares you to respond with compassion instead of defensiveness when real conflicts arise.

Try this:

1. Pick a recent disagreement with your partner.
2. Imagine how they would describe the situation to a friend.
3. Speak their side out loud or write it down.
4. Notice what changes in your understanding.

Journaling Reflections

After that session, Roger took it further. He journaled from the perspective of the woman he'd hurt, not as an apology letter, but as an exploration.

He wrote: "I just wanted to feel like I had a space in your life. It wasn't about the drawer. It was about being welcome. But every time I tried to step closer, you pulled away with a joke. I needed reassurance. What I got felt like rejection."

Journaling in this way helped Roger see his blind spots. It showed him where his fear of closeness came off as coldness. It helped him realize that he wasn't just avoiding hurt—he was hurting others in the process.

You can do the same. Try journaling and ask yourself:

- *What might my partner have felt during that moment?*
- *What fears or needs could they have had that I didn't acknowledge?*
- *If I were them, what would I want me to understand?*

These reflective practices can reveal your assumptions, open emotional insight, and offer unexpected compassion, for both the other and yourself.

Group Discussions

Roger joined a men's group not long after. It wasn't something he would've done in his 30s—too soft, too emotional, too exposed. But now? He was ready to grow.

In that circle, he listened as other men shared similar stories— missed signals, unspoken fears, broken connections. He realized he wasn't alone. More importantly, he practiced staying quiet while others spoke. Not waiting to defend, just listening.

Group discussions like this shift the focus from "me" to "we." They allow you to witness a broader emotional landscape, challenge your default narratives, and build relational empathy across different life experiences.

Whether it's a support group, a workshop, or even deep conversations with friends, stepping into shared emotional spaces can awaken a level of empathy you didn't know you had.

Perspective-taking is a powerful relationship tool. It builds bridges where there were once walls. It turns emotional silence into connection. And as Roger is learning, it's never too late to see the world through another's eyes, and to change how you show up because of it.

Practice Kindness in Everyday Interactions

For most of his life, Roger thought of kindness as something optional—nice to have, sure, but not essential. In his mind, being "straightforward" was more important. He'd say things like "I'm just being honest" when giving criticism, or "Don't take it personally" when brushing off emotional conversations. He didn't realize that the absence of cruelty isn't the same as the presence of kindness. Read that again.

In therapy, Roger began to see how his relationships eroded—not through explosive fights, but through the slow erosion of emotional connection. He never yelled, but he also never noticed. Never celebrated small wins. Never asked about her day with genuine interest. Never brought home her favorite coffee "just because." The kind of gestures that build emotional glue? They weren't part of his daily rhythm.

That's where his growth began: in the daily, quiet, consistent practice of kindness.

Daily Acts of Kindness

Roger's therapist gave him a challenge: one small act of kindness every day. Not flowers or grand gestures. Just simple things: sending a morning text to check in, offering to help a coworker without being asked, or complimenting someone on something they did well.

He started small with his sister, whom he often overlooked. One day, he picked up her favorite almond croissant and left it at her door with a sticky note that said, "Just because I thought of you." She called him later, laughing, and said, "Who are you and what have you done with my brother?"

That moment cracked something open. He realized kindness doesn't just feel good—it creates a ripple of connection. It shifts energy in subtle but powerful ways.

Making Kindness a Priority

It's easy to intend to be kind. It's harder to prioritize it, especially when we're tired, stressed, or triggered. Roger admitted he used to go days without saying anything affirming to the person he was dating. "I assumed they just knew, why else would I be dating them?" he said.

Now, he keeps a sticky note in his wallet: "Be kind on purpose." It's a simple reminder that love isn't passive. It's a choice. A practice.

By intentionally choosing kindness—even when it feels un-
natural at first—Roger began to shift his entire relational
dynamic. He didn't just react to kindness; he generated it. And,
predictably, the people around him responded. More warmth.
More openness. Less tension.

Celebrating Each Other's Successes

In a previous relationship, Roger's partner landed a new job
she was thrilled about. He remembers saying, "That's cool,"
before going back to his emails. At the time, it didn't register.
Now, in reflection, he winces. That moment mattered to her,
and he missed it.

Now, he practices what his therapist calls "enthusiastic presence." When someone shares good news—big or small—he
pauses, asks questions, and celebrates out loud. "That's amazing!" or "You must be proud of yourself—tell me everything!"

Celebrating each other's wins reinforces emotional safety. It
tells your loved ones, "Your joy matters to me." And when joy
is shared, it multiplies.

Kindness in Conflict

Kindness isn't only for the good days. It's especially vital in the
hard ones.

Roger used to get cold during conflict—sarcastic, avoidant,

or distant. But now he's learning that compassion in conflict doesn't mean abandoning your truth. It means delivering it with care.

When he recently had a disagreement with a close friend, instead of withdrawing, he said: "I want to talk about this because I care about you. I know we're both frustrated, but let's figure it out together."

That simple kindness changed the tone completely. Instead of arguing, they collaborated. Instead of escalation, they reached understanding.

Kindness in conflict is a signal. It says, "Even if we don't agree, I still respect you. I'm still here."

Kindness isn't fluff. It's foundational. Roger's story shows us that practicing kindness daily rewires not just how others experience us, but how we experience ourselves. It opens the door to healing, connection, and deeper emotional intimacy.

Develop Active Emotional Listening Skills

Roger always thought he was a good listener. After all, he didn't talk over people, he nodded along, and he could usually repeat back the facts. But what he didn't realize—until therapy— was that emotional listening is a whole different skill. It's not just about hearing words; it's about being present, open, and emotionally available. And in that department? He had a lot of learning to do.

Active emotional listening is one of the most powerful ways to build empathy in relationships. It says, "I see you. I hear you. I care enough to listen with my whole self." And as Roger would come to discover, it can change everything.

Listening Without Interruption

In one of Roger's past relationships, his partner once said, "I feel like you don't really hear me." He immediately responded with, "That's not true—I'm always listening!" Ironically, he had just interrupted her.

His therapist challenged him to try something radical: Say nothing. Let the other person speak until they're finished. Fully finished. No defending. No jumping in to fix it. Just listen.

He noticed that when he didn't rush in to reply, his partner's words changed. They deepened. She felt safer, more seen, and the tension between them softened.

Listening without interruption fosters a space where vulnerability can exist. It allows the speaker to unravel their thoughts, and the listener to absorb, not just respond.

Reflective Listening Techniques

Roger began practicing reflective listening during his sessions. When someone expressed frustration or pain, he'd say things like:

"So, what I'm hearing is that you felt left out when I made that decision without you—is that right?"

Or:

"It sounds like you were really hurt when I brushed you off last night."

At first, it felt a little scripted. But as he practiced, it became more natural and powerful. Reflective listening isn't just repeating words. It's capturing the feeling underneath them. It shows that you're not just hearing their voice, but also their heart.

Roger noticed that when he used this technique with his sister or his coworkers, they opened up more. Conflicts dissolved faster, and the overall quality of the conversation improved.

Recognizing Nonverbal Cues

Roger used to miss things because he was only listening with his ears. Now, he watches closely:

- the pause before a reply
- the way someone fidgets when they're anxious
- how their eyes look away when they're holding back tears

In one conversation with a woman he was dating, she said she was "fine" after an awkward dinner. The old Roger would've taken that at face value. But now, he noticed her clenched jaw, her crossed arms, and the quiet in her voice. So, he said gently, "You say you're fine, but you seem a little distant. Is something bothering you?" She exhaled, relieved. "Yeah... actually, there is."

Being emotionally attuned means tuning in to what's not being said. These non-verbal cues hold emotional weight, and acknowledging them shows depth, awareness, and care.

Practicing Empathetic Responses

Roger's growth became most evident in how he started responding. When a friend shared he was going through a tough divorce, Roger didn't change the subject, crack a joke, or offer unsolicited advice. Instead, he said, "I can't imagine how heavy that must feel. I'm really sorry you're going through this. I'm here if you want to talk more."

It was simple. But it landed deeply.

Empathetic responses validate feelings. They show that you're not just listening; you're feeling with someone. It creates a safe space for honesty and emotional risk.

Roger now knows that empathy isn't about fixing. It's about witnessing. Standing beside someone in their truth and saying, "You're not alone."

Active emotional listening is the foundation of emotional intimacy. You create a powerful emotional connection when you listen without interruption, reflect feelings, notice the unspoken, and respond with compassion.

Roger didn't become an expert overnight. But with every moment he chose to listen—really listen—he rebuilt the emotional bridges he once unknowingly burned. And in doing so, he began to understand love in a whole new way.

Participate in Empathy-Building Activities

Roger never thought of empathy as something you could practice. He assumed you either had it or you didn't—and, if he was being honest, he never saw himself as the "sensitive type." But as he worked through his therapy journey, he realized that empathy wasn't about being soft or emotional. It was about connection. Like any skill worth having, it can be strengthened through experience.

Empathy-building activities offer practical, shared opportunities to connect more deeply—not just with others, but with ourselves. For Roger, these weren't just exercises; they became milestones in his journey from emotional isolation to relational presence.

Volunteer Together

When Roger's therapist suggested volunteering, he resisted. "What does handing out sandwiches have to do with my relationships?" he asked. But he gave it a shot—signing up for a

Saturday food bank shift with a woman he'd just started dating. What surprised him wasn't just how good it felt to help, but how differently he saw her afterward.

He noticed how gently she spoke to an elderly man in line. How she stayed late to clean up. How her eyes lit up when a little girl thanked her.

That day gave Roger a deeper view of her humanity and his own. Volunteering side by side fostered a shared purpose, encouraged mutual appreciation, and gave them something meaningful to reflect on together.

Empathy grows when we step out of our bubble. Service to others helps us recognize common struggles and witness resilience firsthand. It's not just about doing good for others; it's about seeing the world through wider, softer eyes.

Empathy Games

One evening, Roger and his partner attended a community event that included an "Empathy Circle." At first, he rolled his eyes. It sounded like therapy with dice. But the activities were light-hearted and surprisingly impactful. In one game, each person had to role-play the other during a pretend argument. Roger had to voice her side—and she, his.

Suddenly, Roger was saying things like, "I feel invisible when you cancel our plans at the last minute,"—words his partner had actually spoken weeks earlier. And hearing her impersonate his usual "Don't make a big deal out of it" tone? It stung, but it landed.

These games created a safe space for truth and laughter. They made hard conversations easier by putting them into a playful format. More importantly, they helped Roger feel her experience rather than just analyze it.

Empathy games break down barriers, create vulnerability in fun ways, and build emotional fluency in environments that don't feel like pressure cookers.

Workshops or Retreats

Later in his journey, Roger signed up for a weekend emotional intelligence retreat. It was outside his comfort zone—a far cry from his usual solo hikes and sports talk. But something nudged him toward it. Maybe it was loneliness. Maybe curiosity.

The retreat included group exercises on emotional literacy, deep listening, and body language awareness. Roger learned how to sit with discomfort, express his needs without shutting down, and listen without needing to fix.

More powerful, though, was witnessing others do the same. Hearing stories from men and women of all backgrounds opened Roger's heart in ways therapy alone hadn't. He didn't just learn empathy—he felt it in real-time.

Shared learning environments like workshops and retreats

offer concentrated, intentional space for transformation. They give people tools, language, and insight they might never stumble upon alone. And for couples or close friends, they can spark a new chapter of mutual growth.

Empathy doesn't grow in isolation—it thrives in experience. When you volunteer together, play empathy games, or attend workshops that stretch your emotional range, you not only understand others better—you understand yourself better, too.

Final Thoughts: The Empathy Effect

Roger's journey reminds us that empathy and compassion aren't just traits; they're practices. They're choices we make every day, often in small, quiet moments that ripple outward. From pausing to really listen, to volunteering at a food bank, to role-playing an emotional scenario, Roger learned that deeper connection begins the moment we step outside of ourselves and into someone else's experience.

Whether you're trying to heal from past behaviors or build stronger, more meaningful relationships going forward, empathy is the bridge. It softens conflict before it begins, deepens love beyond words, and turns ordinary moments into emotional glue.

But what happens when conflict does arise? Because no matter how empathetic or kind we become, disagreements are part of any real relationship.

That's exactly where we're headed next.

In the upcoming chapter, we'll explore strategies for conflict resolution—not just how to "win" an argument but change it into an opportunity for understanding, healing, and growth. You'll learn techniques to de-escalate tension, communicate your needs without blame, and repair trust when it's been bruised.

Empathy laid the foundation. Now, let's learn how to stand on it—together—when things get tough.

9

Strategies for Conflict Resolution

Chantelle never thought she'd be the kind of woman who yelled at her kids—or snapped at her husband over something as small as a missed text. But here she was: 35, mom of three, new business owner, married to Jim for a decade, and so bone-deep exhausted that even silence felt loud.

Her days were a blur of school drop-offs, work meetings, lost socks, dentist appointments, soccer practices, and last-minute grocery runs. She was constantly needed by someone, somewhere, somehow. And when Jim quietly admitted one night that he was feeling a little neglected—she exploded. Not just a raised eyebrow or a sharp tone. A full-blown, red-faced, tear-laced meltdown.

The truth? Chantelle didn't have a middle. She was either all in or all out. Zero to one hundred. Off or on. When her 13-year-old son gave her teenage attitude, she shouted that he was ungrateful. When her toddler refused to sleep for the third night in a row, she cried in the shower with the water turned all the way up so no one could hear. Her conflict resolution skills? Practically nonexistent. And deep down, she knew her relationships were cracking at the edges.

But she also knew something else: She wanted to change. Not just for Jim. Not just for her kids. For herself.

If you've ever found yourself in Chantelle's shoes—overwhelmed, overstimulated, reactive instead of responsive, feeling like the toxic one—you're not alone. Conflict is part of every relationship, but when you have no resolution skills, it can feel impossible to handle without causing more damage.

This chapter is about doing the hard work of learning how to fight fair, pause before yelling, and get out of the toxic tug-of-war many of us were never taught how to avoid. It's about building practical, real-life strategies to face conflict without crumbling or causing harm.

We'll walk beside Chantelle through some of her toughest moments. We'll dissect what went wrong, and more importantly, what could go right next time. You'll gain insights into your own patterns, learn tools that actually work, and begin practicing healthier ways to handle the heat without burning your relationships to the ground.

Let's begin.

Use Problem-Solving Frameworks

Conflict without a plan is like navigating a storm without a compass. For Chantelle, most arguments start and end in emotional chaos—blame, yelling, guilt, silence. No structure, no solution, just exhaustion. But imagine if, instead of reacting from that survival place, she had a framework to lean on—a map that could guide her through the mess and lead her somewhere better.

Let's walk through four powerful frameworks Chantelle—and anyone—can use to bring more clarity, compassion, and collaboration into conflict.

The Interest-Based Relational Approach

This method is all about solving problems without destroying relationships. It encourages Chantelle not to see Jim—or her teenager—as the enemy, but as a partner in problem-solving.

Instead of focusing on positions ("You never help around the house!" versus "I work all day too!"), this approach invites both people to explore their interests—what they really need. For Chantelle, that might be, "I need to feel supported and not so alone." For Jim, it might be, "I need to feel like I matter to you, too."

When Chantelle stopped to ask, "What are we both trying to get out of this?" she was able to reframe her anger. They

162

both wanted the same thing: connection. This shift—from adversarial to collaborative—helped her cool down and start having conversations that built bridges instead of burning them.

You can protect the relationship while addressing the issue. It's not you vs. me—it's us vs. the problem.

The Six-Step Problem-Solving Process

When conflict feels overwhelming, breaking it into steps can make it manageable. Here's how Chantelle started using this method at home:

1. **Identify the problem:** "We keep fighting at night when we're both tired."
2. **Understand everyone's interests:** "I want peace before bed; Jim wants connection."
3. **List possible solutions:** "Talk earlier in the evening, do a short check-in, leave heavier topics for weekends."
4. **Evaluate the options:** "What actually feels doable with our schedules?"
5. **Select a solution:** "Evening check-in after the kids go down, 15 minutes max."
6. **Agree on next steps:** "Try this for a week, reassess on Sunday."

By laying it out like this, she went from emotional overload to a clear plan, and it worked. Not perfectly, but better. And "better" is a win.

Clarity turns chaos into progress. When you break down the problem, solutions become easier to see and implement.

The Mediation Model

There were times when Chantelle and Jim couldn't even talk without it blowing up. That's when they turned to a counselor— someone trained to mediate, not take sides.

A mediator helped them do something they hadn't done in years: listen. Not wait to respond. Not defend. Just hear each other.

The mediator created a safe space where both of them could speak honestly and be seen. Chantelle admitted how invisible she felt. Jim shared how rejected he felt. That moment of mutual vulnerability cracked the door open to healing.

Sometimes, having a neutral guide makes all the difference. A mediator helps keep things respectful, honest, and productive.

Collaborative Competence

Chantelle realized something big: Conflict doesn't mean failure. It means the relationship is trying to grow. When she stopped trying to "win" arguments and instead focused on teaming up with her husband and kids, everything shifted.

Instead of screaming at her son for leaving dishes out (again), she tried: "I know you're tired, and I am, too. But I need your help. Can we figure out a system that works?" He didn't roll his eyes this time. He actually helped.

Conflict became a chance to practice trust, not break it.

When you focus on team goals, not personal victories, everyone grows. You're not battling each other; you're learning how to solve problems together.

This took time for Chantelle, but she stopped fighting fire with fire. These frameworks gave her something to reach for when her emotions felt too big to handle.

They won't erase every disagreement. But they will help you approach conflict with structure, clarity, and compassion, and that's how healing begins.

Engage in Collaborative Negotiation Strategies

By the time Chantelle hit her 10th married year, her arguments with Jim had started to feel like reruns—predictable, heated, and never really resolved. She wanted help. He wanted connection. But every conversation ended in frustration, with both of them walking away feeling misunderstood.

What Chantelle didn't realize at the time was that she wasn't negotiating—she was debating. And debate has a winner and a loser. What she needed were collaborative negotiation strategies that focused not on winning, but on working together.

Let's walk through how Chantelle—and you—can start turning conflicts into cooperation with four essential strategies.

Finding Common Ground

Chantelle once got into a full-blown argument with Jim about how much time he spent on his phone after work. She was angry because she felt ignored. He was defensive because he felt entitled to a few minutes of peace.

But when they finally sat down without the yelling, they discovered they both wanted the same thing: to reconnect after a long day. That was their common ground.

By starting from shared values—we both care about this relationship   they shifted the dynamic from opposition to collaboration. The moment they could say, "We're on the same team here," their tone changed, their tension eased, and they made progress.

Find the overlap. Even if you disagree on how to get there, starting from a shared goal builds cooperation.

The Win-Win Philosophy

For years, Chantelle saw every conflict as a power struggle. If Jim got his way, that meant she lost. If the kids resisted her rules, it meant they were winning and she was failing. But winning at the cost of connection left her feeling hollow.

The win-win philosophy taught her something different: Real success comes when both sides feel heard, respected, and satisfied.

When negotiating bedtime with her seven-year-old (who wanted to stay up and watch TV), Chantelle tried something new. Instead of laying down the law, she said, "I hear you. How about we do a show together right after dinner, and then we stick to bedtime?" Her daughter beamed. Chantelle got the bedtime she needed. Her daughter got quality time.

A win-win doesn't mean everyone gets exactly what they want, but everyone gets something that matters. That's how you build long-term trust.

Active Listening in Negotiation

In the middle of one particularly heated conversation, Chantelle caught herself doing what she always did: preparing her next comeback while Jim was still talking. No wonder he shut down.

That night, she tried something radical. She didn't speak. She just listened. Not passively—actively. She nodded, para-phrased, and asked clarifying questions. "So, when I forget to text back, it makes you feel invisible?"

He looked surprised, then softened. "Yes. Exactly that."

In that moment, the whole conversation changed. It wasn't about right or wrong; it was about understanding. That made all the difference.

When people feel truly heard, their need to defend or attack fades. Listening creates a space for truth—and resolution—to rise.

Flexibility and Adaptation

Old Chantelle was rigid. Her way or no way. But over time, she learned that clinging to control only deepened conflict.

In one tough conversation about dividing parenting duties, she was dead set on Jim handling all morning drop-offs. He pushed back—it didn't work with his early meetings. Typically, this would've escalated. But this time, Chantelle paused and asked, "What would feel fair to both of us?"

They ended up switching off every other day. Not what either initially proposed, but it worked better than expected.

By loosening her grip, she gained something far more powerful than control: collaboration.

Flexibility isn't weakness; it's wisdom. It opens doors to creative solutions and shows you're invested in the relationship, not just your position.

Chantelle still has moments where she slips into old patterns— don't we all? But she's getting better at recognizing the fork in the road: argue to win, or collaborate to grow.

Conflict doesn't have to be destructive. With collaborative negotiation strategies, it can be the doorway to deeper under-standing, greater intimacy, and real, lasting change.

Learn De-escalation Methods to Manage Disputes

Chantelle used to think conflict meant chaos. Raised voices, slamming doors, and walking away in a swirl of resentment—this was normal, right? It wasn't until her teenage son mim-icked her blowup style during a disagreement that something clicked: She was modeling the very behavior she wanted to stop.

Learning to de-escalate wasn't just about being calmer; it was about being wiser in the heat of the moment. Let's explore the de-escalation techniques Chantelle began practicing and how they can work for you, too.

Techniques for Calming Tensions

There was a moment when Chantelle found herself about to scream at Jim in the middle of a particularly stressful evening—dinner burning, toddler crying, her inbox exploding. Instead, she walked out of the kitchen, closed the door, and took five deep breaths.

It felt strange at first. But when she returned just three minutes later, she wasn't shaking. She could talk instead of explode.

She began building in small calming rituals—stepping outside, holding an ice cube, using box breathing—all tools to pause the emotional storm before it swept her away.

You don't have to resolve everything in the moment. A short pause can save an entire relationship from spiraling in the wrong direction.

Using Neutral Language

Old Chantelle often started with: "You never help me!" or "You always ignore me!" And predictably, those conversations went downhill fast.

Then, she tried something new: "I feel overwhelmed and alone when I'm managing everything by myself."

Same issue. Different language. And the response from Jim? Different, too.

Instead of feeling blamed, he felt invited to understand.

Neutral language—avoiding absolutes, accusations, or loaded terms—became a powerful de-escalation tool in Chantelle's home. It turned confrontations into conversations.

How you say something matters just as much as what you say. Words can either build a bridge or burn it.

Setting Ground Rules for Conflict Discussions

Chantelle and Jim eventually created some simple but sacred conflict ground rules:

- No yelling.
- No interrupting.
- No walking out unless it's to take a short, agreed-upon break.
- Always come back to finish the conversation.

Over time, these rules gave them something they never had before in conflict: a container. A shared understanding that even when emotions ran high, the goal was still respect and resolution.

When Chantelle began applying similar rules with her teen—like waiting until both had cooled off before revisiting the topic—their fights turned into (gasp) actual dialogues.

Ground rules don't make conflict disappear, but they keep it constructive instead of destructive.

Empathetic Responses

"I get that you're frustrated, and that makes sense," Chantelle said quietly to her son one night after he shouted about not wanting to clean his room.

He looked stunned. He expected a lecture. Instead, he got empathy.

And then, surprisingly, cooperation.

Empathy doesn't mean agreement. It means acknowledging emotions—"I see you. I hear you." Chantelle learned that sometimes just validating the other person's feelings took the air out of the anger.

When she used this with Jim—"I know you're feeling shut out right now"—he softened. Defensiveness faded. Problem-solving began.

Empathy isn't weakness—it's leadership in conflict. It deactivates the emotional alarms and clears the way for healing.

De-escalation is about interrupting the cycle of yelling, shutting down, storming off, and regretting it later. Chantelle didn't master these techniques overnight, but each small shift made a huge difference in how her home felt.

And maybe that's the point: You don't need perfect communication. You just need a few tools, some self-awareness, and the courage to change how you show up when it gets hard.

Next time conflict comes knocking, remember: calm isn't weakness—it's power. What's one de-escalation tool you can try today?

Reflect on Conflict Outcomes for Improvement

For a long time, Chantelle's conflicts felt like isolated wildfires—burning hot, leaving damage, and then being quickly buried under busy days. No reflection. No lessons learned. Just survival. But once she started her healing journey, she realized something: If she didn't pause to reflect, she'd just keep repeating the same emotional explosions in slightly different scenes.

Reflection isn't about ruminating; it's about rewiring. Let's explore how Chantelle began using post-conflict reflection to grow stronger, wiser, and more intentional in every relationship.

Post-Conflict Reflection

After a particularly tense exchange with her teenager—one where she raised her voice and he slammed his bedroom door—Chantelle did something different. Instead of storming off or numbing out with her phone, she sat down with a notebook and asked herself these questions:

- *What triggered me?*
- *What did I do well?*
- *What do I wish I had done differently?*

She realized she'd entered the conversation already drained. She hadn't set boundaries around her stress, and her tone came

173

off harsh from the start. That awareness gave her a new plan: Next time, check her energy before engaging.

Reflection isn't about guilt; it's about guidance. The more you learn from the past, the better equipped you are for the future.

Identifying Patterns

Over time, Chantelle began noticing a theme: Almost every major conflict happened when she was overwhelmed, hungry, or feeling unappreciated. These weren't isolated outbursts. They were predictable responses to ignored needs.

By identifying her triggers, she began to build preventative habits: a snack before a tough conversation, a five-minute grounding break, a journal check in when she felt snappy.

She also noticed how her husband often grew silent during conflict. At first, she read it as avoidance. But with reflection, she recognized it as his way of calming himself down. That insight helped her stop taking it personally and start supporting the space he needed.

Patterns reveal what autopilot won't. When you understand your triggers, you gain the power to respond instead of react.

Soliciting Feedback From Others

Chantelle took a brave step: She asked Jim, "How do you feel I handled that last disagreement?" He blinked in surprise, then shared gently, "You stayed calm, which I appreciated, but I felt like you didn't really hear me."

It stung. But it also helped.

She asked her teen, too. "How did I come across just now?" His answer: "Kind of like you'd already decided I was wrong." Ouch. But again—helpful.

Feedback doesn't mean they're right and you're wrong. It means you're willing to grow. By seeking outside perspectives, Chantelle gained valuable insight she couldn't always see from the inside.

Asking for feedback shows you care, not just about being right, but about getting better.

Setting Future Goals

After every major conflict, Chantelle started setting small, achievable goals:

- Next time, pause before raising my voice.
- Let Jim finish his sentence before jumping in.
- Take one mindful breath before speaking when I feel

triggered.

These weren't grand transformations overnight. They were small shifts that added up to something powerful: progress.

Her relationships began to feel less volatile. Her family noticed. So did she.

Goals give your growth a direction. When you know what you're working toward, it becomes easier to walk the path.

Chantelle's reflection didn't stop conflict from happening, but it did stop the same conflicts from happening the same way. She became less reactive, more intentional, and better equipped to handle emotional storms without losing herself in the process.

You can do the same. Look back not to dwell, but to learn. Then, look forward with clarity, compassion, and commitment to doing it better next time.

Final Thoughts: Turning Conflict Into a Catalyst for Change

Chantelle's story reminds us that conflict isn't a sign that something's broken. It's a sign that something needs attention. And with the right tools, even the messiest arguments can become opportunities for growth, healing, and deeper connection.

You've learned that navigating conflict doesn't require perfection. It requires presence. Whether you're using problem-solving frameworks, negotiating with collaboration in mind, de-escalating emotional storms, or reflecting on past moments to do better next time, you're building something powerful: emotional resilience. These skills are your compass when relationships feel stormy.

But conflict resolution is only one part of the equation. It's not just about managing what goes wrong; it's about intentionally creating what feels right.

So, as we move forward, let's zoom out. Let's look beyond arguments and tension, and begin crafting the kind of relationships you actually want to wake up to... forever.

In the next chapter, we'll explore what it means to create a vision for healthy relationships—ones that are rooted in mutual respect, honest communication, emotional safety, and shared joy.

Healing is about more than fixing what's broken. It's about creating what's beautiful.

10

Creating a Vision for Healthy Relationships

Cory is 47. Divorced. A father of two teenagers.

Three years ago, he watched his marriage end not with a bang, but with a slow unraveling—threads frayed from years of conflict, silence, and control. He used to think he was just "direct," "no-nonsense," "the guy who got things done." But the truth was harder to swallow: He was controlling, demanding, and volatile. It was his way or no way. He yelled— loud and often. And when he wasn't yelling, he was emotionally unreachable, shutting down for days at a time, stonewalling anyone who tried to reach him.

It wasn't that he didn't care. It was that he didn't know how to care in a healthy way. He had no idea how to name what he was feeling, let alone say it out loud. Vulnerability wasn't in his vocabulary—power was. Control was. And underneath all of it? Fear.

It took years of therapy, soul-searching, a divorce, and a few breakdowns before Cory finally saw it clearly: His behavior wasn't just about being "stubborn" or "hot-tempered." It was rooted in something much deeper: abandonment.

Cory was given up by his birth mother at birth. He bounced through foster homes like a pet no one wanted to keep. Every time he started to trust, he was moved. Every time he needed something, he learned to silence it. He believed—deep down— that people leave. That love is conditional. That if you want to stay safe, you stay in charge.

But all that guarding cost him. It cost him connection, peace, and eventually, his marriage.

And yet—this isn't a story about what Cory lost. It's a story about what he chose to rebuild.

Today, Cory has three clear goals:

1. To strengthen the co-parenting relationship with his ex-wife. He doesn't want this to come from guilt, but out of love for their children and respect for the family they once were.
2. To show up as the kind of father he never had. The kind who listens. Who apologizes. Who teaches through actions, not just advice.
3. To grow a new kind of love in his current relationship. One that doesn't punish, hide, or dominate but collaborates, adapts, and communicates.

He's not perfect. Triggers still sneak in. Old fears still knock. But now, he sees them. He names them. He talks about them. He chooses new ways forward—sometimes messy, but always honest.

And that's where this final chapter begins.

You've already done the heavy lifting. You've confronted your own toxic behaviors. You've developed the tools to change. Now, it's time to look ahead and ask:

What kind of relationship do I truly want to build from here?

Whether you're single, partnered, co-parenting, or still healing, this chapter is about crafting a personal and shared vision for what healthy looks like. Not perfect. Not performative. Just honest, loving, and aligned with who you're becoming.

Let's build that vision—together with Cory—and lay down the foundation for lasting, fulfilling connections.

Ready? Let's begin.

Envision Relationship Goals Through Visualization

Understanding Visualization

You've probably heard the phrase "You must see it to believe it." When it comes to building healthier relationships, it's more than a catchy saying—it's a strategy backed by both science and soul.

Visualization is the practice of mentally picturing your desired outcomes as if they're already happening. It's not about wishful thinking or fantasy. It's about creating clarity. It's about emotionally connecting to the kind of love and partnership you want to create so deeply that your heart starts to lead the way.

Let's go back to Cory.

After years of therapy and self-reflection, Cory didn't just write a list of goals—he started to visualize what success looked like in each of them. Every morning, he'd take five quiet minutes to imagine the following:

- sitting across from his ex-wife, calmly co-parenting with respect and ease, putting their kids first
- sharing a meal with his son and daughter, being fully present, not reactive, laughing more, teaching through warmth instead of control
- being with his new partner in tough moments—not shutting down, not raising his voice, but taking a breath, expressing his fear rather than letting it explode as anger

He saw these moments in his mind before he lived them. And over time, his body and brain began to follow the path he envisioned. His nervous system felt safer. His communication softened. His choices started aligning with his vision because he knew what he was aiming for.

Here's why visualization works:

- It helps you clarify your personal relationship goals by moving beyond abstract wants (like "I just want peace") and into vivid emotional detail (like "I want to come home and feel emotionally safe with my partner after a hard day").
- It creates internal motivation. When you can feel what that healthy relationship looks like—even for a few seconds—you become more committed to making it real.
- It builds emotional resilience. When setbacks happen (because they will), that clear mental picture gives you something to return to—a lighthouse in rough emotional seas.
- And perhaps most importantly, it reminds you that you're in the driver's seat. You're not waiting to be rescued or for someone else to fix it. You're creating your future with intention.

Now, it's your turn.

Start small. Visualize one moment of connection that you'd like to create in your life. Maybe it's a peaceful dinner without tension. A conversation where you feel truly heard. A moment where you express love, even when it's uncomfortable. Close your eyes. See it. Feel it. Live it, in your mind, before you live it in your world.

Visualization is more than a practice; it's a promise to yourself.

And the more you keep that promise, the closer you get to

building the relationship you've worked so hard to deserve.

Creating a Vision Board

Sometimes, seeing is more powerful than saying. While visualization happens in the mind, a vision board brings those mental images to life, turning abstract desires into something you can look at every single day.

A vision board is a tangible, creative way to express your relationship aspirations. It's not just a collage of pretty pictures—it's a mirror of your intentions. And for someone like Cory, who once struggled to name his feelings at all, the act of making a vision board became a surprisingly powerful step in his healing.

At first, Cory thought the idea sounded a bit childish—cutting out magazine photos and gluing down words like connection and trust. But his therapist encouraged him to approach it as an emotional exercise, not an art project.

So, he gave it a try.

He invited his kids to do it with him—an open, unexpected moment of bonding that gave them insight into his growth. They sat at the kitchen table on a rainy Saturday, flipping through magazines and laughing, talking about what they wanted their family to feel like. His daughter picked a picture of a father hugging his kid. His son added the word respect in bold black letters. Cory chose images of a peaceful home, a couple communicating over coffee, a man journaling near a mountain.

Then, a week later, he invited his new partner to make a separate board with him—one that reflected their shared relationship values. They added words like honesty, repair, and playfulness. It wasn't about perfection. It was about vision.

Here's why vision boards matter:

- They help you consolidate your thoughts and emotions about what you truly want in your relationships, both with others and with yourself.
- They create a daily visual reminder that keeps your goals top of mind. It's easy to slip back into old habits. But it's harder to ignore your commitments when your board is staring back at you from the wall or fridge.
- They're adaptable. As you grow, your board can evolve. You can add, edit, or start a new one to reflect deeper goals or stronger boundaries. It's a living document of your personal growth and relational intentions.

And maybe the best part? You don't have to do it alone.

Like Cory, you can invite your kids, partner, or even close friends into the process. Because when you involve the people you love in your vision, you're not just telling them who you want to be—you're showing them.

So, grab some scissors, magazines, markers—or go digital if you prefer. It doesn't have to be fancy. Just honest.

This is your opportunity to put your heart on paper and create a map for the kind of love you're ready to build.

Guided Prompt: How to Create Your Relationship Vision Board

You don't need to be an artist or a Pinterest pro. All you need is honesty, curiosity, and a little time to reflect on the kind of relationships you want to grow—from romantic partnerships to parenting, friendship, or self-love. Here's how to bring it all to life:

Set the mood: Find a quiet space or invite people you trust to join you. Light a candle, play music, or make tea—whatever helps you feel relaxed and open.

Reflect on these prompts: Before you begin cutting or clicking, take a few minutes to journal or simply think through these questions:

- *What qualities do I want in my relationships?* (e.g., honesty, laughter, growth, emotional safety)
- *How do I want to feel with the people closest to me?*
- *What kind of partner/parent/friend do I want to be?*
- *What behaviors or habits am I committed to changing or nurturing?*
- *What does "healthy love" look like to me?*

Gather your materials: Choose a format that feels right:

- Paper version: Grab scissors, glue, old magazines, newspapers, or printed photos. You'll need a poster board or a large sheet of paper.

· Digital version: Use Canva, Pinterest, Google Slides, or a collage app on your phone/tablet.

Find and collect your images and words: Look for images, colors, and words that resonate with your vision. You might include the following:

· a couple laughing or problem-solving together
· the word "repair" or "presence" or "trust"
· a picture of a dinner table, symbolizing connection
· a photo of a calm forest, representing emotional peace
· quotes about growth, love, or self-awareness

Arrange and create: There's no wrong way to build your board. Let your intuition guide you. Maybe one side is for romantic relationships and another for family. Maybe it's all blended together. Go with what feels meaningful.

· **Place it where you'll see it often:** Your vision board is a daily reminder of what you're working toward. Place it somewhere visible: your bedroom wall, closet door, fridge, or digital wallpaper.
· **Revisit and revise over time:** This is a living, breathing reflection of your goals. As you grow, so can your board. Revisit it monthly or seasonally. Add to it. Change it. Let it evolve with you.

Journaling About Future Relationships

Visualization can help you *see* the kind of relationship you want, but journaling helps you understand it.

Journaling about future relationships gives you space to explore your desires in detail, uncover your deeper needs, and get honest about what truly brings you joy, peace, and connection. Writing slows the mind down just enough for clarity to emerge. And sometimes, what you think you want on the surface isn't what your heart is quietly asking for.

Cory learned this the slow way.

At first, journaling felt awkward. What was he supposed to write? A grocery list of romantic wishes? But his therapist encouraged him to treat it as a letter to his future self or even a letter to the kind of partner he wanted to become.

So, Cory began writing about this:

- what emotional safety looked like.
- how he hoped his next argument would feel different than past ones.
- what kind of father he wanted to be remembered as.
- how it would feel to be in a relationship where love wasn't earned by control, but offered freely through trust.

In doing this, he realized that happiness in his relationships wasn't about avoiding conflict; it was about creating a space where truth could exist without fear.

Here's what journaling can do for you:

- encourage introspection—helping you dig beneath surface-level desires and into your real emotional needs
- clarify essential relationship values, like trust, safety, freedom, and fun
- provide insights about compatibility—you begin to notice patterns in what you're asking for and what red flags you want to avoid
- support emotional awareness—especially when reflecting on past pain or hopes for future healing

Try this prompt to start: *In my ideal relationship, I feel... We handle disagreements by... I show love by... My partner makes me feel... We grow together by...*

Revisit your answers often. Your desires may shift as you grow, and that's the whole point.

Guided Visualization Exercises

To deepen your journaling practice, try pairing it with a guided visualization. This structured mental exercise helps you not only picture your future relationship but feel your way into it, offering powerful insight into your needs and responses.

Cory did this as part of his healing journey. One night, after a tough moment with his new partner where he almost fell back into old habits, he sat down, closed his eyes, and imagined the same scene—only this time, responding with calm, vulnerability, and empathy.

He pictured

- taking a breath instead of raising his voice.
- saying, "I feel scared right now" instead of withdrawing.
- his partner reaching out, not recoiling, because she felt safe, too.

When he opened his eyes, he felt a soft ache in his chest—a mix of grief for past moments lost and hope for future ones he could still create.

That's the power of guided visualization. It allows you to

- explore different relationship scenarios with emotional honesty.
- assess your emotional reactions—what feels exciting, scary, or deeply aligned.
- build an inner roadmap for how you want to act and feel when challenges arise.

Try this simple guided visualization:

1. Sit comfortably. Close your eyes. Breathe deeply.
2. Picture a future moment in a healthy relationship—maybe it's a Sunday morning, a tough conversation, a celebration, or a quiet evening at home.
3. What do you *feel* in your body? What emotions are present?

How do you and your partner interact?
4. What choices do you make that reflect your growth?
5. Stay in the moment for a few minutes. Then open your eyes and write about it in your journal.

This practice doesn't just help you dream; it helps you prepare. It invites your nervous system, emotions, and awareness to start showing up as the person you want to be in love.

Set Realistic Aspirations for Relationship Growth

When you've done a lot of healing work, it's easy to swing from one extreme to the other. You've come through the fire— now you want your next relationship (or current one) to be the picture of perfect communication, zero triggers, and constant harmony.

But growth doesn't need to be perfect—it needs to be possible.

Cory learned this the hard way.

After years of confronting his own toxic behaviors, he stepped into his new relationship ready to "get it right." He'd read the books, done the therapy, written the journal entries. But then a stressful week hit: His partner pulled away, his teens were acting out, and he caught himself defaulting to old habits: shutting down, getting short, trying to control what he couldn't.

At first, he spiraled. "I've done all this work—why am I still messing up?"

But with help, Cory realized he wasn't failing. He was facing a new level of the work. And most importantly, his goals needed adjusting. Not lowering, but grounding.

Understanding Realistic Goals

Setting realistic aspirations means recognizing what's *truly possible* right now—for yourself, your partner, and your situation. It's not about shrinking your vision, but about pacing it.

Cory shifted from "I'll never raise my voice again" to "When I feel triggered, I'll pause and name the feeling." He shifted from "We'll never argue" to "We'll disagree respectfully and return to repair quickly." He stopped expecting his ex-wife to perfectly co-parent and instead focused on creating consistency in their communication and supporting their kids through change.

These small shifts didn't lower the bar—they made it reachable. And reaching that bar over and over built trust, safety, and momentum.

Here's why realistic relationship goals matter:

- Unrealistic expectations often lead to disappointment, shame, or resentment when we or others fall short.
- Realistic goals create sustainable progress. They're less flashy but more powerful over time.
- Incremental improvement is how real change happens.

Tiny moments of growth build a new normal.

Assessing Current Relationship Health

Before setting goals, it helps to take an honest look at where things stand now. What's working? What's struggling? What needs attention, grace, or courage?

Cory started doing this check-in monthly, with himself and, sometimes, with his partner. He asked himself questions like:

- *When was the last time I felt truly connected to my kids or partner?*
- *What's one thing I handled better this month than I would have a year ago?*
- *What pattern is starting to show up again—and what's it trying to teach me?*

This helped him stay grounded in the real relationship, not the idealized one in his head. It allowed him to spot progress and tweak goals without shame.

A few reflection questions you can ask yourself:

- *What strengths already exist in my relationship(s)?*
- *What are the recurring challenges or triggers?*
- *Am I expecting too much too soon from myself or my partner?*
- *Where can I offer more compassion—to them and to me?*

Growth isn't about a finish line; it's about direction.

When you set goals that match your current reality and stretch you just a little past it, you give yourself the best chance to build something lasting, loving, and authentic.

Collaborative Goal Setting With Partners

Healing yourself is powerful. But building something healthy with someone else?   That's where the real magic—and challenge—happens.

Healthy relationships aren't built by one person doing all the work. They're co-created through shared vision. When both people are involved in shaping the goals and direction of the relationship, they're more likely to feel connected, understood, and motivated to grow together.

That's something Cory had to learn.

In his marriage, he never invited collaboration. He made the decisions. He dictated the tone. And when things got hard, he either shut down or took over. His voice was the loudest—not necessarily because he was right, but because he didn't trust anyone else to care the way he did.

But in his new relationship, Cory decided to do it differently. One night, instead of hiding after a tense disagreement, he initiated a vulnerable conversation. He asked, "What kind of relationship do you want to build together? And what do you need from me to feel safe in it?"

It wasn't easy, and it didn't wrap up in one evening. But over time, they began setting goals together:

- taking a walk each week to check in emotionally
- practicing a 10-minute "pause" when a conversation gets heated
- sharing gratitude out loud before bed
- supporting each other's personal growth, not just the relationship's growth

Why does this matter?

- Shared goals strengthen the bond. It feels like a team, not a test.
- Mutual understanding builds emotional safety—you both know what matters most.
- Joint commitment minimizes conflict because you're both rowing in the same direction.

If you're in a relationship, invite your partner into the vision-making process. It doesn't need to be formal. Just start with curiosity:

- "What does a healthy relationship mean to you?"
- "What do you want more of between us?"
- "What would progress look like in how we handle hard days?"

Remember: Setting goals together isn't about forcing alignment; it's about finding shared meaning.

Adapting to Change

No matter how clear your goals are, life will get messy.

People change. Circumstances shift. And relationships—if they're to last—must bend without breaking.

Cory experienced this firsthand. Just as he and his partner were hitting a rhythm, his ex-wife moved to a new city with the kids. Co-parenting changed overnight. His schedule shifted. Emotions flared. Old fears of being left behind resurfaced.

At first, Cory panicked. This wasn't the plan. But instead of clinging to rigid expectations, he took a breath and did what the old version of himself never would have done: He adjusted.

He and his partner revised their goals. Less in-person time with the kids meant more intentional virtual connection. They let go of some structured routines and focused on emotional flexibility—checking in more often, giving grace on the days that felt off.

Here's the truth:

- Change is inevitable. Holding tightly to outdated goals creates stress and disconnection.
- Flexibility invites growth. When you allow your relationship to evolve with life's seasons, it becomes more resilient.
- Regular reflection keeps you aligned. Checking in every few months about goals, feelings, and values ensures your

relationship is still moving in the direction you both want.

Try asking this:

- "Are our current goals still relevant to our lives right now?"
- "Have either of our needs shifted?"
- "What do we need to release, revisit, or reaffirm?"

Relationships thrive when we grow together—honestly, intentionally, and with room to adapt.

Cory didn't become the perfect partner, but he became a present one. One who listens, adjusts, and builds alongside the people he loves.

And that's the kind of love worth envisioning and co-creating.

Identify Steps to Achieve Relationship Happiness

Healing is the beginning, but happiness in a relationship? That comes from the steps you take, daily, to nurture connection, growth, and shared joy.

Relationship happiness doesn't appear overnight. It's built slowly, through effort, reflection, and showing up for each other, especially when it's inconvenient. It's about progress, not perfection.

Let's look at how Cory turned his growth into daily practice and how you can too.

Creating Action Plans

After his divorce, Cory knew what he wanted: to co-parent with peace, to be an emotionally present dad, and to thrive in a healthy new relationship. But knowing wasn't enough. He needed a plan.

With the help of his therapist, Cory broke his big goals into small, repeatable actions. Here are some examples:

- Instead of "be a better dad," he set the goal of spending 20 minutes of distraction-free time with each child twice a week.
- Instead of "communicate better," he practiced saying "I feel..." instead of "You always..." during tense conversations.
- Instead of "don't shut down," he committed to telling his partner when he needed space—and returning to the conversation within 24 hours.

These weren't grand gestures. But they were clear. And they added up.

These action plans work because

- they help translate abstract goals into tangible steps.
- they keep you accountable—you know what to do and how often.
- they create momentum, helping you stay motivated through small wins.

Action Plan Template

Here's a simple template to help you build your own relation-ship action plan:

Use this chart to define 2–3 goals that align with your vision. Keep it visible: on the fridge, in your journal, or shared with your partner.

Establishing Healthy Communication Routines

Cory used to shut down for days when he felt overwhelmed. Now, he and his partner have a weekly check-in—just 20 minutes to share feelings, review goals, and name anything unsaid.

Sometimes it's lighthearted. Sometimes it's uncomfortable. But it's always a moment of intentional connection.

Routines like this matter because

- they prevent misunderstandings from festering.
- they normalize vulnerability and emotional transparency.
- they give both partners a chance to feel heard and sup-ported.

Start with a simple routine: Every Sunday evening, we'll sit down for 15 minutes and ask:

- "How did we do this week?"
- "What's something I appreciated about you?"
- "Is there anything we need to work through?"

Celebrating Small Wins Together

Cory's partner used to remind him: "Notice the little stuff."

So, they started celebrating even the tiniest progress: a disagreement handled calmly, a heartfelt compliment, a day with no silent shutdowns.

They'd say things like, "Hey, we did that differently today and it worked." Or they'd high-five after a shared parenting win. Sometimes, they just lit a candle and had wine to toast a good week.

Small celebrations matter because

- they keep the relationship positive and energized.
- they affirm that progress is happening, even if it's slow.
- they build a habit of mutual appreciation, which strengthens connection.

Try creating your own ritual:

- a weekly "win jar" where you both drop in something you're proud of
- a monthly celebration night for any relational growth
- a simple text during the day that says, "I noticed what you

did—and I'm grateful"

Seeking Support When Needed

Cory didn't do it alone. He had therapy. His kids had a family counselor. He and his partner joined a couples workshop together.

Because he knew: Even with all the tools, sometimes you need a guide.

Support makes growth sustainable. It helps you understand, not just react. It reminds you that your relationship isn't broken; it's evolving.

Seeking support can look like

- seeing a couples therapist or relationship coach.
- joining a parenting group or support circle.
- listening to podcasts or reading together about emotional intelligence, healing, or intimacy.
- having honest conversations with trusted friends who model healthy relationships.

As Cory says, "I thought asking for help meant I was failing. Now I see it means I'm serious about doing this right."

Happiness in relationships doesn't come from the absence of problems. It comes from the presence of effort, awareness, and love in motion.

Start where you are.

Take one step.

Celebrate it.

Ask for help when you need it. And keep building, just like Cory, one honest moment at a time.

Final Thoughts: Your Vision, Your Future

By now, you've done what many never dare to do: You've faced your patterns. You've owned your pain. You've made space for healing. And now, you've imagined something better—something healthier, more honest, and more aligned with who you are becoming.

This final chapter asked you to get clear. To be brave enough to say, "This is the kind of relationship I want to build, and here's how I'll start showing up for it."

Just like Cory, you've probably seen how messy healing can be. But also how deeply rewarding it is to replace old habits with conscious choices—to stop reacting and start creating.

Whether you're rebuilding a relationship, starting a new one, or still healing from the last, your vision matters. It becomes your compass. It helps you choose love on purpose, with clarity and care.

Carry this forward:

- Keep visualizing.
- Keep journaling.
- Keep speaking your truth.
- Keep adjusting as you grow.
- Keep celebrating the small wins.

You don't have to do it alone, and you don't have to get it all right the first time.

Because the most powerful part of any relationship isn't the past; it's the vision you carry into the future.

Here's to the relationships you're about to build—rooted in honesty, nourished by intention, and sustained by love that evolves with you.

You've done the work. Now, go live the vision.

11

Conclusion

Full Circle

Let me take you back to where this all began.

Yes—that ex.

The one I was married to for over a decade. The one I laughed with, cried with, built a life with—and eventually, unbuilt one with, brick by emotional brick.

When our marriage ended during the pandemic, I thought it was the end of everything that mattered. In some ways, it was. But what I didn't know at the time—what only distance and deep reflection could teach me—was that it was also the beginning of something new, something more whole.

The truth is, heartbreak cracked me open. And the light

that poured in didn't just illuminate my pain—it revealed my patterns, my wounds, and most importantly, my capacity to grow. And that growth has led me here—to a place I never imagined I'd be.

I'm friends with my ex.

And not in the vague, polite-texts-on-birthdays way. But in a real, honest, mutual-respect kind of way. We support each other. We show up for our shared history with humility, not hostility. We're not what we once were. We're something new. Something we built by healing separately and choosing to relate differently.

That journey—from bitterness to clarity, from blame to accountability, from pain to peace—is what inspired this book. And if you're reading these words right now, it means you've been walking that journey, too.

So, let me pause here and say something important:

You did something brave.

You didn't just pick up this book—you finished it. That alone deserves a moment of recognition. Because this wasn't light reading, it was soul work.

You've dared to look at yourself, not just the parts you like, but the ones you've hidden, denied, or felt ashamed of. And instead of running, you stayed. You read. You reflected. You owned it. And you took steps toward becoming the version of yourself that your future relationships—and your current self—deserve.

Let's take a moment to look at all you've walked through:

- You identified your own toxic behaviors, not to shame yourself, but to understand them.
- You explored your attachment style and how your past has shaped your patterns.
- You learned how to manage anxiety, silence overthinking, and show up with emotional regulation.
- You practiced new communication tools—assertiveness, active listening, empathy, and repair.
- You learned to spot red flags in others and yourself.
- You revisited past wounds, not to reopen them, but to release what no longer serves you.
- You built emotional intelligence, not as a buzzword but as a skillset to love more deeply and safely.
- You embraced boundaries, not as walls but as invitations to healthy connection.
- You cultivated compassion, not just for others but for the wounded parts of yourself.
- You developed strategies for resolving conflict, creating vision, and sustaining intimacy.

You built your toolbox. You wrote your vision. You dared to dream of a future that looks nothing like your past. That's no small feat.

You did this.

You made space for healing. You chose awareness over autopilot. You picked up the mirror and used it not to criticize, but to understand.

And now, whether you're starting fresh, rebuilding something familiar, or still choosing yourself day by day—you are equipped.

Let's be honest: The work isn't over. It never really is. But that's okay. Healing isn't a finish line. It's a way of walking.

And the more you walk this way—with curiosity, compassion, clarity, and courage—the more you become the kind of person who can give and receive the love you've been looking for.

The fact that you're here means you're already becoming that person.

And maybe, like me, you'll find yourself one day sitting across from someone you shared mutual hurt with and realizing that your story didn't end where the pain began. It just had to take a detour through growth.

That's the beauty of this work. It rewrites the ending.

Thank you for letting me walk this path with you. It has been an honor to be your guide, your witness, and your companion in these pages.

If this book supported your journey—if even one chapter sparked a shift—I'd be so grateful if you'd consider leaving a review. Your feedback not only helps others find the book but reminds fellow travelers that they're seen, heard, and worthy.

From my heart to yours—thank you. For showing up, staying open, and choosing healing, even when it hurt.

Here's to your vision, your voice, and the relationships you are about to build.

You are not behind, you are on your way. And your future is already thanking you for the work you're doing right now.

Keep going.

With you in the journey,
   —*Matt*

Bonus Content

I have created valuable bonus content to support your journey with "How to Stop Being Toxic."

Using the QR code below will take you to a site where you can claim your bonuses.

The bonus content includes:

- **21-Day Toxic Pattern Breaking Challenge**: Daily actions designed to interrupt toxic cycles and build healthy communication habits that stick
- **Toxic Behavior Communication Scripts**: Ready-to-use conversation templates for addressing past harm, setting boundaries, and repairing relationships with authenticity
- **Toxic Behavior Emergency Intervention Kit**: Immediate techniques to redirect toxic impulses before they damage your relationships

To collect your bonuses:

- Open your camera app.
- Point your mobile device at the QR code that follows.
- This will take you to a landing page where you can claim

your bonuses.

Or you can go to this link in your web browser:

https://subscribepage.io/QgWGEB

I hope you find this content useful in your personal journey to let go and I wish you every success.

About the Author

Accomplished author Matt Tomporowski writes transformative self-help books and his blog, *Chasing Dreams in Middle Life*, to support readers in their emotional well-being and personal development. His mission is to help readers lead happy and healthy lives.

Through his writing, he enables people to break free from limiting patterns and beliefs, guiding them toward happiness and fulfillment. His approach combines clinical research with practical, accessible strategies for lasting change. Matt's work aims to help others release emotional baggage and create lives filled with purpose and joy.

Join Matt on his ongoing journey and discover more insights on his Substack blog "Chasing Dreams in Middle Life" at https://matttomporowski.substack.com/

Also by Matt Tomporowski

"LETTING GO RIGHT NOW"

The breakthrough guide to clearing your mind and eliminating negative thinking.

Are you ready to break free from what's holding you back?

In "Letting Go Right Now," Matt Tomporowski shares practical wisdom, science-backed techniques, and actionable strategies to help readers:

- Clear their minds of persistent negative thoughts

- Release emotional attachments that no longer serve them
- Develop powerful mindfulness practices for daily life
- Create an action plan for moving forward with confidence
- Transform how they respond to life's challenges

This easy-to-read guide combines inspiration, scientific insights, and step-by-step exercises designed to help individuals overcome what's holding them back and embrace a more fulfilling life.

Available now in print, e-book, and audiobook formats.

Scan the QR code below or visit https://mybook.to/Letting_Go_Right_Now to learn more about "Letting Go Right Now" on Amazon.

References

References

Apostolou, M. (2022). Should I stay or should I go? Behavioral acts that negatively affect relationships' prospects. *Evolutionary Psychology*, 20(4). https://doi.org/10.1177/14747049221134220

Barkley, S. (2024, October 8). *The cycle of dysfunctional relationships*. Psych Central. https://psychcentral.com/relationships/why-do-we-repeat-the-same-dysfunctional-relationship-patterns

Charlie Health Editorial Team. (2023, April 28). *Toxic relationships & mental health*. Www.charliehealth.com. https://www.charliehealth.com/post/how-toxic-relationships-affect-your-mental-health

Cherry, K. (2023, December 31). *5 key components of emotional intelligence*. Verywell Mind. https://www.verywellmind.com/components-of-emotional-intelligence-2795438

Feuerman, M. (2024, November 19). Managing vs. resolving conflict in relationships. *The Gottman Institute.* https://www.g

ottman.com/blog/managing-vs-resolving-conflict-relations
hips/

Friedman, G. (2021, May 18). Understanding avoidant attachment in relationships. *Power Couples Education.* https://powerc
oupleseducation.com/blog/avoidant-attachment-style
    George, E. (2024, May 31). *Triggers.* MentalHealth.com.
    https://www.mentalhealth.com/library/understanding-trig
gers

Gunther, R. (2021, September 15). 9 qualities of the most
successful relationships. *Psychology Today.* https://www.ps
ychologytoday.com/ca/blog/rediscovering-love/202109/9-qu
alities-the-most-successful-relationships

Gupta, S. (2024, April 18). *What does secure attachment look and
feel like? Plus how to develop it.* Verywell Mind. https://www.ver
ywellmind.com/secure-attachment-signs-benefits-and-how
-to-cultivate-it-8628802

How to improve your emotional intelligence. (2019, August
26). Professional Development | Harvard DCE; President and
Fellows of Harvard College. https://professional.dce.harvard.e
du/blog/how-to-improve-your-emotional-intelligence/

Koniver, L. (2022). Practical applications of grounding to
support health. *Biomedical Journal*, 46(1). https://doi.org/1
0.1016/j.bj.2022.12.001

Leaf, C. (2021, October 31). The difference between toxic and
healthy boundaries. *Dr. Leaf.* https://drleaf.com/blogs/news/b

oundaries?srsltid=AfmBOoo8WlkIDg95aclM3BFB-iR86udseA
gklNQ8doxRqfuTVKuKBKop

Lisitsa, E. (2024). The four horsemen: Criticism, contempt,
defensiveness, and stonewalling. In *The Gottman Institute*.
https://www.gottman.com/blog/the-four-horsemen-recogni
zing-criticism-contempt-defensiveness-and-stonewalling/

Martin, S. (2020, April 23). 7 types of boundaries you may need.
Psych Central. https://psychcentral.com/blog/imperfect/2020/
04/7-types-of-boundaries-you-may-need

McLachlan, S. (2014, October 10). Collaborative negotiation –
6 important reminders about this win-win approach. *Thought
Exchange.* https://thoughtexchange.com/blog/collaborative-n
egotiation-6-important-reminders-about-this-win-win-ap
proach/

Miller, M. (2021, January 8). *Getting unstuck: The power of
naming emotions.* Six Seconds. https://www.6seconds.org/
2021/01/08/getting-unstuck-power-naming-emotions/

Nakao, M., Shirotsuki, K., & Sugaya, N. (2021). Cognitive–behavioral therapy for management of mental health and stress-
related disorders: Recent advances in techniques and technolo-
gies. *BioPsychoSocial Medicine*, *15*(1), 1–4. https://doi.org/10.11
86/s13030-021-00219-w

Nelson, K. (2025, March 5). *How an anxious attachment style
can impact a relationship "...are you still there?"* Verywell Mind.
https://www.verywellmind.com/navigating-relationships-wit

h-an-anxious-attachment-style-in-the-21st-century-52250
19

Powell, A. (2018, April 9). *Harvard researchers study how mindful-ness may change the brain in depressed patients.* Harvard Gazette; Harvard University. https://news.harvard.edu/gazette/story/2 018/04/harvard-researchers-study-how-mindfulness-may-change-the-brain-in-depressed-patients

Shifting her experience. (2020, September 21). *Do you have toxic traits? How to identify your own toxic behaviors.* Medium. https://shiftingherexperience.medium.com/do-you-have-tox ic-traits-how-to-identify-your-own-toxic-behaviors-30e00 12a5036

Smith Haghighi, A. (2024, September 26). *Types of therapy: For anxiety, depression, trauma, PTSD and more.* Www.medicalnews today.com. https://www.medicalnewstoday.com/articles/type s-of-therapy#animal

Souza, M. D. (2024, May 9). *How to know if you're a toxic person.* Marcellodesouza.com.br. https://www.marcellodesouza.com.b r/how-to-know-if-you-are-a-toxic-person/

Sutton, J. (2018, May 14). *5 benefits of journaling for mental health.* Positive Psychology. https://positivepsychology.com/b enefits-of-journaling/

Sutton, J. (2021, November 9). *Conflict resolution in relationships and couples: 5 strategies.* PositivePsychology. https://positiveps ychology.com/conflict-resolution-relationships/

Tomporowski, M. (2025, March 25). From heartbreak to friendship: The unexpected journey after divorce. *Chasing Dreams in Middle Life.* https://matttomporowski.substack.com/p/from-heartbreak-to-friendship-the?
  r=fk82p&utm_campaign=post&utm_medium=web&triedR edirect=true

Verma, M., Rathore, M., Nirwan, M., Trivedi, S., & Pai, V. (2022). Functional connectivity of prefrontal cortex in various meditation techniques – A mini-review. *International Journal of Yoga*, *15*(3), 187–187. https://doi.org/10.4103/ijoy.ijoy_88_22

Walker, S. A., Pinkus, R. T., Olderbak, S., & MacCann, C. (2023). People with higher relationship satisfaction use more humor, valuing, and receptive listening to regulate their partners' emotions. *Current Psychology*, *43*. https://doi.org/10.1007/s 12144-023-04432-4

Made in United States
North Haven, CT
31 July 2025

71167435R00124